W9-DHI-790

The Fourth Dimension
of a Poem

and Other Essays

M. H. ABRAMS

The Fourth Dimension
of a Poem

and Other Essays

FOREWORD BY Harold Bloom

W. W. NORTON & COMPANY
NEW YORK · LONDON

For information about permission to reproduce
selections from this book, write to
Permissions, W. W. Norton & Company, Inc.,
500 Fifth Avenue, New York, NY 10110

For information about special discounts for bulk
purchases, please contact W. W. Norton Special Sales
at specialsales@wwnorton.com or 800-233-4830

Manufacturing by Courier Westford
Book design by Brooke Koven
Production manager: Devon Zahn

Library of Congress Cataloging-in-Publication Data

Abrams, M. H. (Meyer Howard), 1912–
The fourth dimension of a poem : and other essays /
M.H. Abrams ; foreword by Harold Bloom. — 1st ed.
p. cm.
Includes bibliographical references and index.
ISBN 978-0-393-05830-7 (hardcover)
1. Poetry—History and criticism. 2. Poetics. I. Title.
PN1031.A27 2012
808.1—dc23

2012020169
W. W. Norton & Company, Inc.
500 Fifth Avenue, New York, N.Y. 10110
www.wwnorton.com

W. W. Norton & Company Ltd.
Castle House, 75/76 Wells Street, London W1T 3QT

1 2 3 4 5 6 7 8 9 0

for Jane and Judy

CONTENTS

FOREWORD

by Harold Bloom

1

ON JULY 23, 2012, my revered mentor Meyer Howard Abrams will turn exactly a century old. At noon today, February 5, I phoned him to say I was writing this foreword, and rejoiced to hear him sounding zestful and vigorous.

In September 1947, an awkward boy of seventeen, I edged into my first class at Cornell University. My teacher, a calmly cheerful man of thirty-five, was Mike Abrams, as he is universally called. Shy and rather fearful, I gazed at him with instant affection and awe, impulses that continue strongly sixty-five years later.

Without his teaching, his personal guidance, and his extraordinary patience with me, I would have capsized well before freshman year came to a close. My passion for learning, and in particular for appreciating authentic poetry, went back to early childhood, and I had the advantage of preternatural speed in reading, accompanied by total memorization of what moved me most, whether in prose or verse. But socially I scarcely existed, hindered by self-consciousness and acute anxieties.

I am now in my fifty-sixth consecutive year of teaching at Yale University. One element in my refusal to retire is my career-long sense that I want to do for my students what Mike Abrams accomplished with me. For temperamental reasons, I never have, yet must go on trying. His serenity is hopelessly beyond me, but I think back to it and gradually have learned to subdue some aspects of my personality so as to listen intently to my students when they most need adequate response.

I will devote the rest of this brief foreword to Abrams' intellectual and scholarly achievement in his writings, yet had to begin with homage to his splendor as a teacher, always humane and humanistic. What emerges in all of his published work is a secular faith in disciplined imagination and high aesthetic standards. He continues the tradition of the ancient Hebraic sages. I think of Hillel in particular: "Be deliberate in judgment, raise up many disciples, and build an open enclosure around the Torah," which for Mike Abrams is the Western literary canon. As his disciple, I try to emulate him.

2

Abrams' masterwork is *The Mirror and the Lamp: Romantic Theory and the Critical Tradition* (1953), which retains its freshness and clarity. It traces the two paths of critical theory, the classical as founded by Aristotle, and the Romantic, inspired by Longinus, until their mingled culmination in the high Romantics Samuel Taylor Coleridge, Percy Bysshe Shelley, and William Hazlitt.

I purchased my prime teacher's *The Mirror and the Lamp* on February 24, 1955 (the date is inscribed upon it), during my Fulbright year at Pembroke College, Cambridge, where I was finishing my Yale doctoral dissertation on Shelley. Going through it now, I see it is covered with penciled-in marginalia, written across fifty-seven years of rereading. At one point today I found in a margin the seeds of what many years later was to develop into my brief book *The Anxiety of Influence*, though Mike is not to be held culpable for my kabbalistic elaborations.

His other grand work is *Natural Supernaturalism: Tradition and Revolution in Romantic Literature*, which he gave me in June 1971, the year of its publication. Powerfully, *Natural Supernaturalism* chronicles the displacement of religious formulations by high Romantic speculations and visions, in an array of thinkers and poets from St. Augustine through Hegel on to Blake, Wordsworth, Carlyle, and D. H. Lawrence, among many others.

Looking through my forty years of copious marginalia, I find my own awakening to the secularized epiphany or privileged moment, which led me to Walter Pater, and to my subsequent critical reflections on the continuity between Romantic tradition and the twentieth-century poets I most admire: W. B. Yeats, Wallace Stevens, D. H. Lawrence, and Hart Crane.

Mike Abrams has published several other books, the most admirable being *The Correspondent Breeze: Essays on English Romanticism* (1984). Its major essay is "Structure and Style in the Greater Romantic Lyric." Here my marginalia are profuse, and explore the affinities of Mike's establishment of a poetic genre with my own ruminations on the modern crisis-poem, from William Collins on to Hart Crane.

The Fourth Dimension of a Poem and Other Essays, to be published for Mike's one hundredth birthday, moves me by its vibrancy and humane charm. Here I desire to comment only on the final essay-review, which is of David Bromwich's superb first book, *Hazlitt: The Mind of the Critic* (1983).

I had the pleasure and honor of being Bromwich's teacher at Yale, but he arrived fully formed, the Hazlitt of his generation, and scarcely needed me. This was very different from my relation to Mike Abrams, who had to free me from many doubts and persuade a very rough, rather inchoate social self that it could qualify for an academic and literary critical career.

I give the final paragraph of Mike's essay-review, and the close of this volume, so as to begin an appropriate grace note for celebrating the Abrams Centennial:

> Hazlitt, himself an athlete, describes the elements and relations in his ideal of prose by a trope taken from athletic contests: "Every word should be a blow, every thought should instantly grapple with its fellow." When he is at his best in expressing the supple energy of his mind in the power of his prose, Hazlitt makes De Quincey's craftsmanship in the essay seem ponderous, Leigh Hunt's lightweight, and even Lamb's, in many instances, sequestered and quaint. There are moods of reading, in fact, in which no other essayist can give us the satisfaction that Hazlitt does. R. L. Stevenson said in one of his essays that "though we are mighty fine fellows nowadays, we cannot write like Hazlitt." David Bromwich, in the opening paragraph of his book about the other Hazlitt, cites this comment as appropriate to the standard Hazlitt, about whom he remarks that "I never cared for him much." I have a hunch, though, that even the other Hazlitt would have liked Stevenson's compliment very much.

Stevenson was right: no other critic in English, not even Dr. Samuel Johnson, matches the power of Hazlitt's prose. Last year I reread nearly all of Hazlitt, searching for answerable style in my old age. I memorized again many passages that had become shadowy recollections, but one in particular stays with me, so that sometimes I murmur it to myself during sleepless nights:

> Surely, if there is anything with which we should not mix up our vanity and self-consequence, it is with Time, the most

independent of all things. All the sublimity, all the superstition that hang upon this palpable mode of announcing its flight, are chiefly attached to this circumstance. Time would lose its abstracted character, if we kept it like a curiosity or a jack-in-a-box: its prophetic warnings would have no effect, if it obviously spoke only at our prompting like a paltry ventriloquism. The clock that tells the coming, dreaded hour—the castle bell, that "with its brazen throat and iron tongue, sounds one unto the drowsy ear of night"—the curfew, "swinging slow with sullen road" o'er wizard stream or fountain, are like a voice from other worlds, big with unknown events. The last sound, which is still kept up as an old custom in many parts of England, is a great favourite with me. I used to hear it when a boy. It tells a tale of other times. The days that are past, the generations that are gone, the tangled forest glades and hamlets brown of my native country, the woodman's art, the Norman warrior armed for the battle or in his festive hall, the conqueror's iron rule and peasant's lamp extinguished, all start up at the clamorous peal, and fill my mind with fear and wonder. I confess, nothing at present interests me but what has been—the recollection of the impressions of my early life, or events long past, of which only the dim traces remain in a smouldering ruin or half-obsolete custom. That *things should be that are now no more*, creates in my mind the most unfeigned astonishment. I cannot solve the mystery of the past, nor exhaust my pleasure in it.

("On a Sun-Dial" [1827])

Regret hardly could be phrased more eloquently or plangently. I recall that I first read "On a Sun-Dial" for one of Mike's classes, and treasured his comments upon it, one of which stressed the strength of: "Time, the most independent of all things." Abrams, a great scholar-teacher, approaches his one hundredth birthday with an autonomy that yields nothing to time. In my own lifetime of battling incessantly against all vagaries and fashions that threatened to dehumanize aesthetic education and criticism, I have relied implicitly upon Mike Abrams as my sage and fathering force, and I am only one of many.

The Fourth Dimension
of a Poem

and Other Essays

The Fourth Dimension of a Poem

"The Fourth Dimension of a Poem." To explain that enigmatic title, I'll begin by quoting the opening paragraph of a novel written while its author was teaching at Cornell:

> Lolita, light of my life, fire of my loins. My sin, my soul. Lo-lee-ta: the tip of the tongue taking a trip of three steps down the palate to tap, at three, on the teeth. Lo. Lee. Ta.

Humbert Humbert's obsession with Lolita has sensitized him to a fact to which we are ordinarily oblivious; that is, that the use of language involves a physical component, the oral actions of producing the words we utter, and that by attending to them,

---

This was a lecture delivered at several universities in 2010–11. The text is that of the version delivered at Cornell in November 2010. The lecture relies on oral demonstrations of the diverse effects of the enunciated speech-sounds that constitute the words of a poetic passage. A video of the lecture at Cornell is available online at fourthdimensionofapoem.com.

we can become aware of the mobile and tactile sensations of performing these actions. The point I want to stress is that poets, whether deliberately or unconsciously, exploit the physical aspect of language. It is this component—the act of its utterance—that I call the fourth dimension of a poem.

There are, one can say, four dimensions that come into play, to produce the full effect of reading a poem. One dimension is its visible aspect, which signals that you are to read the printed text as a poem, not as prose, and also offers visual cues as to the pace, pauses, stops, and intonation of your reading. A second dimension is the sounds of the words when they are read aloud; or if they are read silently, the sounds as they are imagined by the reader. A third, and by far the most important dimension, is the meaning of the words that you read or hear. The fourth dimension—one that is almost totally neglected in discussions of poetry—is the activity of enunciating the great variety of speech-sounds that constitute the words of a poem.

It is easy to overlook the fact that a poem, like all art forms, has a physical medium, a material body, which conveys its nonmaterial meanings. That medium is not a written or printed text. The physical medium is the act of utterance by the human voice, as it produces the speech-sounds that convey a poem. We produce those sounds by varying the pressure on the lungs, vibrating or stilling the vocal cords, changing the shape of the throat and mouth, and making wonderfully precise movements of the tongue and lips. It can be said, then, that the physical production of a poem begins next to the heart and ends near the brain. That is one reason that poetry is felt to be the most intimate of the arts, in addition to being the most inclusive and nuanced in expressing what it is to be human. I want to emphasize how important it is to become aware of this fourth, material dimension of a poem. Lifelong and constant habituation in using language has made us largely oblivious to the oral activities that bring a poem into being—the sensations of motion, shape, and touch that we feel, and the oral gestures that we make, in performing such activities; but to be oblivious to these physical sensations and gestures, and simply to look through them to the meanings of the words that they convey, is to disembody a poem. An important advantage of reading a poem aloud is that to do so helps to reembody it, by emphasizing the palpability of its material medium. And that is important, because the oral actions that body forth the words of a poem, even when they remain below the level of awareness, may serve, in intricate and diverse ways, to interact with, confirm, and enhance the meanings and feelings that the words convey.

What I have said will, I think, become more clear after I discuss some poems, then read them aloud. But before I do so, I want to stress that there is no one right way to read a poem aloud. Good readers vary greatly, and even the same reader does not read a poem twice in precisely the same way. I go back far enough so that, when I was a college student, I heard T. S. Eliot, Ezra Pound, and e. e. cummings read their poems; each read differently, but all read well. I heard Robert Frost talk his poems, to great effect; and I heard Dylan Thomas recite poems in a Welsh bardic chant, to equal effect. In the early decades after the founding of Cornell, a famed English professor, Hiram Corson, read poems aloud in Sage Chapel accompanied by the chapel organ, to high acclaim.

I myself favor a more subdued mode of reading—a flexible one that subordinates itself to, and tries to express and convey, the physical as well as the semantic particularities of an individual poem. To illustrate, I shall point out some of the distinctive qualities of each of six poems, then read it aloud. I chose these examples because they are all splendid poems, of which I am especially fond, yet differ markedly in the implied voice of the lyric speakers, in what the speakers say, and the style and pace and tone in which they say it. I will attend to all four dimensions of these poems, but will emphasize especially their fourth dimension—that is, the differences in the physical, enunciative actions which help the poems achieve their varied effects, by interacting with the meanings and moods that the words of the poems convey.

1.

W. H. Auden, "On This Island" (1936)

"On This Island" was written by W. H. Auden at the age of twenty-eight, in an exuberant display of his early mastery over the resources of language. Most prominent is his use of devices—especially the emphatic repetition of stressed syllables, and the conspicuous patterning of speech-sounds—that he had learned from the poet-priest Gerard Manley Hopkins. Almost all of Hopkins' poems, although written in the high Victorian period, had not been published until 1918, only eighteen years before "On This Island"; and Hopkins' linguistic innovations captivated Auden, as they did other young poets of his generation.

Auden's poem represents the sea and shore as overlooked from, presumably, a chalk cliff on the southeast coast of the large island called Great Britain. "Look, stranger"—the poet addresses himself directly to you, whom the poem thus posits as a fellow viewer of this vibrant scene, drenched in sunlight and resonant with the sounds of ever-moving water. Conspicuously in this representation, Auden exploits all four of the poem's dimensions—its visible appearance, its speech-sounds, its meanings, and also its fourth dimension, the act of its utterance—and makes them cooperate so as to convey to the full the sights, motions, and sounds of this sunlit seascape, as well as the exhilaration that the view evokes in its observer.

Throughout his description, Auden makes us aware of something we ordinarily are oblivious to—the delight that can reside in mere utterance, in our uniquely human ability to enunciate an astonishing variety of speech-sounds. Infants show this delight in the activity called "lalling"—that is, the repetitive utterance of newly learned consonants: *ma-ma-ma-ma, da-da-da-da, la-la-la-la*. Auden recovers for us, on a complex level, this lost primitive pleasure. For example, he bids us to look at

> —this island now
> The leaping light for your delight discovers.

In representing the dazzle of the light (which seems to leap up from the moving waters that reflect it), Auden matches the delight he experiences in viewing the represented scene by the delight he evokes in our oral activities of verbalizing that representation—delight in the repeated utterance of the elastic *l*'s, and in the evolution of the speech-units, from "leaping" to "light" to "delight" to "discovers" ("the leaping light for your delight discovers"). The restless movements, both in the scene and in its verbal representation, are brought to an abrupt stop by the sturdy sequence of stressed *st*s in the imperative to you, the listener, to "*St*and *st*able here." In that last phrase, Auden exploits the potential semantic content of uttering the initial *st*'s—a combination of consonants that recurs in many English words that denote a sudden cessation of movement, in words such as "*st*op," "*st*ay," "*st*uck," and "*st*ock-*st*ill"; "Stand stable here."

Such a prominent play of speech-sounds is not only pleasurable in itself, but has an additional function; and that is, to replicate the sounds that the words signify. For example, in "The swaying sound of the sea" (the last line of the first stanza), which describes the rise and fall in loudness of the sound of the sea swells, the sibilance of the enunciated *s*'s mimics the

susurrus of the sliding waters, at the same time that the undu-
lating rhythm of the spoken line—most prominent in the pressure and release of the medial *y* in the word "swaying"—mimics
the undulation of the waves that produce those sounds. Auden
also reminds us, by using oral echoism, that at the sea's edge,
the waves do not merely hiss. As they strike the shore, they also
make slapping and clicking sounds (line 9):

> —and its tall ledges
> Oppose the pluck
> And knock of the tide. . . .

In the lines that follow, Auden foregrounds something that he
also does, less obviously, elsewhere in the poem. He has learned
from Gerard Hopkins the trick of breaking a word in the middle
and then rhyming the first half of the severed word with the end
word of a nearby verse line:

> —oppose the pluck . . .
> —after the suck-
> ing surf. . . .

By this device Auden makes us aware that in uttering words we
perform oral gestures, and that such gestures can be meaningful. In this instance, he breaks the word in order to emphasize
a change of direction in the gesture of enunciating its speech-
sounds, from the front to the back of the mouth in "suck-", then
from the back to the front of the mouth, to end far forward, with
the labiodental *f*: "the suck- / ing surf." In these lines, therefore,
even as the speech-sounds—the *s*'s and *f*'s and *k*'s—reproduce
the diverse sounds we hear at the margin of the sea, the reversal
of motion in enunciating the speech-sounds enacts the reversal
in motion of the surf that the words signify, as the wavelets reach

up on the shore, stop, and then, reluctantly, revert to the open sea: "suck / ing surf."

One more comment, to show how Auden exploits all the dimensions of his poem, including its visual appearance on the page. Each of the three stanzas contains a remarkable variety of line lengths, consisting of two, three, four, and five iambic units, or feet; but in nonnumerical order. In the first two stanzas, for example, the order of the line lengths is four, five, two, two, four, three, and three metric units. When you read these lines aloud, the varying lengths of their uttered sound mimic the irregularity in the sounds made by the varied reach of the individual waves as they impinge on the shore. But Auden knows also that we ordinarily encounter a poem visually, in a printed text. Accordingly, he uses the irregular pattern of this visual aspect of the poem, as you see it on the page before you, to replicate the irregular visual pattern that is etched on the sandy shore by the advancing and retreating waves.

I must emphasize that Auden's poem is a great deal more than a linguistic tour de force. Note what he says in lines 5 and following:

> That through the channels of the ear
> May wander like a river
> The swaying sound of the sea.

In this passage Auden attributes to the consciousness of you, the perceiver, a spatial dimension, into which the oscillating water-sounds enter, as though the sounds were themselves water that flows through your ear canal (the "channels of the ear") into your conscious mind. And even more remarkably, in the third line of the last stanza:

> And the full view
> Indeed may enter

> And move in memory as now these clouds do,
> That pass the harbour mirror
> And all the summer through the water saunter.

As the moving clouds are reflected in the water, so "the full view"—full, because it includes both the water and the moving clouds that are reflected in the water—is in turn reflected in the perceiver's consciousness, where the clouds continue to move, but now in the perceiver's memory. In both these intricate metaphoric figures, the outer is fused with the inner, so that the scene and the seer, the human perceiver and the natural things that are perceived, are assimilated into a single perceptual whole.

A final comment about this remarkable little poem. In the third line from the end, Auden introduces five sequential stresses—"And move in memory ás nów thése clóuds dó"; he then lengthens the concluding line from three feet (as in the two preceding stanzas) to five feet: "And áll the súmmer thróugh the wáter sáunter." He does so in order to make both the length and the metric pace of these descriptive lines accord with what they denote—that is, with the sustained, unhurried pace of the moving clouds that are reflected in the water. But beyond this: the last two lines are, surely, among the loveliest in English poetry. In part what we perceive as the beauty of their sound is in fact a projection, from the act of utterance onto the resulting sounds, of the pleasurable ease with which we are able to enunciate the succession in these lines of their frontal consonants. More important to the effect, however, is that these two lines contain a sequence of no less than five two-syllable trochaic words, all of which rhyme, but on the off beat only: "hárbŏur," "mírrŏr," "súmmĕr," "wátĕr," "sáuntĕr." The oral act of producing these recurrent half-rhymes—the fourth dimension of these lines—is the more delightful, because Auden makes us sense also the feel of enunciating the nasal continuant *m*'s in "mirror" and "summer," then to move to the contrasting plosive *t* in "water," and to conclude with the combination of both nasal and plosive in the *nt* of that perfectly apt word, in its utterance, its sound, and its sense: the artfully delayed, indolent verb, "saunter." May I ask you to read these last two lines of the poem aloud with me, in order to savor the evolution of their contrasting speech-units?

> That pass the harbour mirror
> And all the summer through the water saunter.

Did you taste those consonants?

Well, you're standing on the top of a chalk cliff when the poet turns to you:

> Look, stranger, at this island now
> The leaping light for your delight discovers,
> Stand stable here
> And silent be,
> 5   That through the channels of the ear
> May wander like a river
> The swaying sound of the sea.
>
> Here at the small field's ending pause
> Where the chalk wall falls to the foam, and its tall ledges
> 10   Oppose the pluck
> And knock of the tide,
> And the shingle scrambles after the suck-
> ing surf, and the gull lodges
> A moment on its sheer side.
>
> 15   Far off like floating seeds the ships
> Diverge on urgent voluntary errands;
> And the full view
> Indeed may enter

And move in memory as now these clouds do,

20   That pass the harbour mirror

And all the summer through the water saunter.[1]

2.

Emily Dickinson, "A Bird Came Down the Walk" (1862)

We turn to Emily Dickinson's poem, which, in contrast to Auden's extensive seascape, is an exquisite piece of minute description. "My Business," Dickinson wrote in a letter, "is Circumference"; by which cryptic statement I take her to mean that she circumscribes a small area of observation, then explores its minutiae.

In this poem, a robin dispatches a worm, hops about, and then, when offered a crumb, flies off. That's all. Dickinson makes of the robin's negotiation with the worm, and of its actions after that, a comic pantomime in miniature; while of the bird's final flight— well, how is one to describe what she does in this astonishing passage of verbal impressionism? The act of the bird unfurling its wings and taking off, and of an oarsman rowing so gently as to leave no trace in the still water, and of butterflies launching themselves silently in order to float through the air, are so inter- fused, and the elements of air and water so commingled, that the bemused reader ceases to know—or to care—which words are literal and which are metaphorical.

In part, what we sense as the delicate adaptation of Dickinson's words to what they describe is the result of their fourth dimen- sion—the actions of enunciating them. In the last two lines of the fourth stanza, for example—

And he unrolled his feathers

And rowed him softer home—

eight of the ten words have prominent components—denoted by the letters *h*, *th*, *w*, and *f*—in which the sound is produced by applying a soft pressure that forces the air through constricted oral passages—

> And *h*e unrolled *h*is *f*ea*th*ers
> And ro*w*ed *h*im so*f*ter *h*ome

These oral actions accord with, and so enhance, the actions they describe; and that is, the soft pressure on the air by the robin's wings as he unrolls his feathers and flies—or rows, or swims—away.

Within this floating suspension of equated utterances and actions, butterflies are said to leap from banks. We expect, in this watery context, that these are the banks of a stream. But no; they turn out to be the banks of an abstraction, a time of day—"Noon." In this dislocation of concentrated reference, I can compare Dickinson to only one prior lyric poet, William Blake, at his audacious best.

> A Bird came down the Walk—
> He did not know I saw—
> He bit an Angleworm in halves
> And ate the fellow, raw,
>
> 5   And then he drank a Dew
> From a convenient Grass—
> And then hopped sidewise to the Wall
> To let a Beetle pass—
>
> He glanced with rapid eyes
> 10   That hurried all around—

They looked like frightened Beads, I thought—
He stirred his Velvet Head

Like one in danger, Cautious,
I offered him a Crumb
15   And he unrolled his feathers
And rowed him softer home—

Than Oars divide the Ocean,
Too silver for a seam—
Or Butterflies, off Banks of Noon
20   Leap, plashless as they swim.[2]

If it were all we had, this one poem would be enough to establish Emily Dickinson's genius. Fortunately, we have many hundreds of her writings. To be precise, she left in manuscript at
her death seventeen hundred and seventy-five poems. Of these,
an astonishing number are comparable in excellence to the one
before us.

3.

William Wordsworth, "Surprised by Joy" (1815)

In a note Wordsworth tells us that "Surprised by Joy" has reference to his daughter Catherine, who had died a year earlier
at the age of four. It was written when Wordsworth was in his
mid-forties, in the demanding form of the Petrarchan sonnet,
and its language has something of the stiff formality that dead-
ens much of the poetry Wordsworth wrote in his middle and
later age. But what makes this poem the more moving is that
the speaker's spontaneous overflow of powerful feelings breaks

into and disrupts the formality both of its language and of its intricately rhymed stanza.

Surprised by a circumstance that gives him joy, the poet instinctively turns (and we turn with him) to share his feelings with his little daughter. But the second line is interrupted by the interjection "Oh!" and the word "whom" at the end of the line forebodes its rhyme-word, "tomb." In a stab of pain, he remembers that she is dead. He consoles himself that his habitual act of turning to her to share his joy attests the fidelity of his love. Then the anguished outcry: "But—how could I forget thee?" What these broken lines convey is a deeply human paradox about grieving. Time is a healer; but the dimming of grief in the passage of time can make us feel guilty, as though it impugned the depth of our love. In the sharpness of his self-blame, the poet (in the fourth dimension of his language) belabors himself with a barrage of blunt, bilabial *b*'s—how "have I *b*een so *b*eguiled as to *b*e *b*lind / To my most grievous loss!" To realize that he has momentarily forgotten the pain of his loss is the greatest pain he's ever known. But no; once more he has to correct himself—the worst pain, diminishing with the passing of time, was that he suffered when he first knew that his daughter was gone, forever.

> Surprised by joy—impatient as the Wind
> I turned to share the transport—Oh! with whom
> But Thee, deep buried in the silent tomb,
> That spot which no vicissitude can find?
> 5   Love, faithful love, recalled thee to my mind—
> But how could I forget thee? Through what power,
> Even for the least division of an hour,
> Have I been so beguiled as to be blind
> To my most grievous loss!—That thought's return
> 10 Was the worst pang that sorrow ever bore,

> Save one, one only, when I stood forlorn,
> Knowing my heart's best treasure was no more;
> That neither present time, nor years unborn
> Could to my sight that heavenly face restore.

In a poem written to memorialize Wordsworth's death in 1850, Matthew Arnold said that the unique quality of Wordsworth's poetry was its "healing power."

> But where will Europe's latter hour
> Again find Wordsworth's healing power?

In our present critical climate, that is not the kind of thing one is apt to say about poems. But surely, Arnold's claim comports with our response to "Surprised by Joy" and with our response to Wordsworth's great narrative poems about suffering, *The Ruined Cottage* and *Michael*. In his sonnet, Wordsworth confronts the most terrible of bereavements, the death of a beloved child, yet transmutes it for his readers into an experience of comfort—of comfort and even a kind of joy; the kind we call aesthetic delight. He does so because he achieves—and enables us to do so too—a mode of mastery over grief, by finding language greatly adequate to its occasion. He does so also by reassuring us that we are not alone, that we share with this insightful poet the perplexities of our human condition.

4.

Alfred, Lord Tennyson, "Now Sleeps the Crimson Petal" (1847)

In lyric poetry the most frequent topic is, of course, love. But in the two thousand-plus years of recorded amatory poems, I know none that quite matches Tennyson's "Now Sleeps the Crimson

Petal." Tennyson's popularity with the Victorian middle class is unexampled in the history of poetry; but the truth is, proper Victorians had nothing against amatory poems. To the contrary—provided the poem is discreet in its language, and lacks overt physical references. Tennyson's poem qualifies on both these counts, but barely.

"Now Sleeps the Crimson Petal" is, in its unobtrusive way, a poem of total, unmitigated, suspenseful sexual longing. Its setting, we learn, is an opulent palace garden, which contains red and white rose bushes, cypress trees, and goldfish in a rich stone bowl. The garden adjoins a lake in which grow day-blooming water lilies, and (the ultimate exotic touch) it harbors a white peacock. Night has at long last descended, lit only by fireflies and the luminous track of a shooting star. The lyric speaker is waiting for his beloved to waken and join him in this rich, fragrant, breezeless darkness. As we are told in the sixth line of the poem, the beloved keeps this rendezvous: "And like a ghost she glimmers on to me." The pronoun "she" in that line can't refer to the peacock, which is a male peafowl; what the line conveys, then, is that the loved one herself appears, her white dress glimmering, ghostlike, in the darkness. All the while, the lyric speaker's perfervid imagination transforms every detail that he perceives into an analogue of his desire.

Though lacking rhyme, the lyric is divided into stanzas, made up of an opening and closing quatrain (four lines) and four intervening couplets. Each stanza is demarcated by opening with the temporal adverb "now" and ending with the personal pronoun "me." The cumulative effect is of the sustained urgency of a desire so intense that it induces in the lover a physical languor: "Now, now, now, now, now"; "with me," "to me"; "unto me," and then twice: "in me," "in me."

The second of the insistent couplets contains what I would nominate as, in a discreetly indirect way, the most explosively concentrated erotic image in all poetry: "Now lies the Earth all Danaë to the stars." In Greek mythology Danaë is a young woman whose father, to ward off her suitors, has locked her behind bars; but the amatory Zeus, chief of the gods, in the standard euphemism "visits" her in a shower of gold. Just unfold Tennyson's compressed allusion, and it turns out to convey something like this: by the tensely expectant lover, all the earth is perceived as though it were an enamored female, lying receptive to the multitudinous silver showers of the visiting stars. "Now lies the Earth all Danaë to the stars."

Note now the first line of the concluding quatrain. The normal word order would be "Now the lily folds up all her sweetness." By inverting the subject and predicate and postponing the preposition "up" until the end, Tennyson suspends the syntactical closure so as to replicate the suspense of the waiting lover: "Now folds the lily all her sweetness up." By delaying the closure, Tennyson also heightens our awareness of what it feels like to terminate the clause by enunciating the plosive *p* in the word "up"; and that in turn makes us aware of the repetition of that speech-sound in the following verb "slips," and then of the repetition of that word, in the final request to his loved one: "slip / Into my bosom. . . ."

I draw your attention to another, and very important, aspect of an expressive utterance of a poem. Tennyson's verse quickly establishes as its basic meter five iambic feet per line, with each foot taking up an approximately equal segment of time. "Nŏw sléeps thĕ crímsŏn pétăl, nów thĕ whíte." If the utterance reproduced metronomically these stresses and time intervals, it would be lethal to the poem. Instead, a sensitive reading plays counterpoint to the normative meter, so that its intonation—that is, the expressive changes, in uttering the poem, of pitch, pace, pause, and rhetorical stress—sometimes deviates from, sometimes coincides with the pulse of the underlying meter. This dynamic of tension and resolution between the normative meter and an expressive rendering is what gives vitality to a poem when it is uttered aloud.

As example, take the opening line. When reading it, I at one time stressed rhetorically the opposing adjectives "crimson" and "white": "Now sleeps the crímson petal, now the whíte." But that was clearly a mistake. The difference between white and red roses is not functional to the import of the poem. The keynote term is "now," which, in consequence, though it lacks a metrical stress, invites an intonational stress, "Nów sleeps. . . ." Equally important, however, is the verb "sleeps"—"Now, at last, at last, the darkness falls, so that the red rose *sleeps*." Here the intonational stress conjoins with, so as to reinforce, the metrical stress on "sleeps." In this longed-for darkness, when the rose finally sleeps, the firefly wakens. And now at last, at last, it's time for my love also to waken, to keep her rendezvous, in the still darkness of this garden, with me.

So throughout the poem: an expressive utterance manifests a counter-rhythm that plays with and against the underlying metric pulse. And as recurrently earlier, so at the very end, the metrical and the intonational stresses coincide; the poem thus concludes with a plangent double emphasis on the sentient center of all this suspenseful longing—"me."

> Now sleeps the crimson petal, now the white;
> Nor waves the cypress in the palace walk;
> Nor winks the gold fin in the porphyry font.
> The firefly wakens; waken thou with me.
>
> 5   Now droops the milk-white peacock like a ghost,
> And like a ghost she glimmers on to me.
>
> Now lies the Earth all Danaë to the stars,
> And all thy heart lies open unto me.

Now slides the silent meteor on, and leaves
10   A shining furrow, as thy thoughts in me.

Now folds the lily all her sweetness up,
And slips into the bosom of the lake.
So fold thyself, my dearest, thou, and slip
Into my bosom and be lost in me.

5.

Ernest Dowson, "Cynara" (1891)

I have been inordinately fond of Ernest Dowson's "Cynara" ever since, as a susceptible college sophomore, I came across it in a survey course in English literature. I like it not despite, but because of, its extravagance. The subject of the poem is outrageous, deliberately intended, in 1891, to shock the late-Victorian reader. The lyric speaker, during a long night of dissipation, and while lying in the arms of a prostitute (note in the second stanza "her bought red mouth"), is obsessed with the memory of an earlier love, and asserts that this obsession, in these circumstances, proves his fidelity to that loved one. I find appealing the candor with which Dowson flaunts his poem's high artifice. He begins with an epigraph from a Latin ode, in which the poet Horace, referring to a former love, declares, "I am not as I used to be, under the reign of the good Cynara"; Dowson then appropriates the name of Horace's mistress for his own lost love. The artifice is highlighted by the intricacy of the six-line stanza, in which five of the lines are written in iambic hexameter—a six-stress meter that is rare and difficult to sustain in English without monotony. The poet, however, interpolates in each stanza a fifth line, which is shortened from six to five stresses, and is made additionally plangent because it intersects the two-line refrain and its resounding rhyme of "passion" with "fashion."

Dowson is really a masterful metrist. Take, for example, in the opening line of the second stanza, the sequence of six stressed syllables—"Í félt hér wárm héart béat." The effect of uttering these words is to make you feel each individual throb of her warm heart. And immediately following, we get the two strong sequential stresses in the phrase "Níght lóng"; here, the effect of the act of utterance is to convey, by mimicry, the length of that night of love.

To mention one more example of Dowson's exploitation of the enunciative dimension of language: in the second and third lines of stanza 3, note the suspension in the juncture between those two lines, forced by the need to re-form the vocal organs from the *ng* to the *d*, in the adjacent stressed syllables "throng" and "dancing." We must move from the back of the tongue at the roof of the mouth, to the front of the tongue just above the teeth. The suspension, effort, and release in the enunciative action mimics the bodily action when we dance—

> Flung roses, roses riotously with the thróng,
> Dáncing. . . .

That dance, by the way, was very likely a Viennese waltz, a somewhat scandalous dance that was all the rage in 1891, when Dowson wrote "Cynara." And what about this possibility? Immediately after the word "dancing" we find a succession of four *l*'s, each formed by the pressure and quick release of the blade of the tongue against the roof of the mouth—

> Dancing, to put thy pa*l*e *l*ost *l*i*l*ies out of mind.

The final *l* in "pale," however, merges with the initial *l* in "lost," and also gives it added emphasis. The result, in the act of utterance, is a sequence of three syllables beginning with *l*: "*l*ost *li*lies—*ló li li*—1-2-3. The enunciated syllables mimic the triple beat and swing of the Viennese waltz.

If someone were to object that, in this instance, I claim too much for the fourth dimension of Dowson's language, I would have to confess that I half agree with him. But be that as it may, I am confident that the riotous dance Dowson had in mind was a Viennese waltz. It is significant that in 1885, six years before "Cynara," Dowson's friend and fellow poet Oscar Wilde had published "The Harlot's House." The setting of this poem is an upper-class bordello in which the patrons are dancing wildly to an orchestra playing what the poem explicitly identifies as a waltz by Johann Strauss.

Prominent throughout Dowson's "Cynara" is the unabashed theatricality—even staginess—of its high rhetoric and broad gestures, which would be at home in a lush Victorian melodrama: "Last night, ah, yesternight"; "Yea, I was desolate." And in the third stanza, "I have forgot much, Cynara! gone with the wind. . . ." Yes, that's where Margaret Mitchell got the title for her Civil War novel. Incidentally, from this poem derives also the recurrent phrase in verses by that very literate songwriter, Cole Porter. Do you remember?

> I'm always true to you, darling, in my fashion,
> I'm always true to you, darling, in my way.

Such literary echoes reassure me that I'm not the only reader to have been beguiled by Dowson's flamboyant poem.

Despite its patent contrivances, "Cynara," it seems to me, escapes being meretricious or insincere; instead, the very candor of its artifice generates a kind of authenticity, building up to the outcry in the fifth, shortened line of the last stanza: "Yea, hungry for the lips of my desire." In rendering this line, as in the rest of the poem, the reader is licensed—indeed, required—to be histrionic, but must take care not to slip into self-parody. Such restraint is made easier—and the poem is also made much more interesting—by the teasing phrase that closes each stanza, and lingers in memory when the poem ends: "in my fashion." How is one to take those words? Clearly, they indicate the speaker's awareness of the extravagance of his claim; but do they suggest also a touch of self-mockery? Well, that depends on the interpretation by the individual reader, as that interpretation is expressed by the intonation the reader gives to the phrase, especially at the close of the final stanza.

Non sum qualis eram bonae sub regno Cynarae

Last night, ah, yesternight, betwixt her lips and mine
There fell thy shadow, Cynara! thy breath was shed
Upon my soul between the kisses and the wine;
And I was desolate and sick of an old passion,
5   Yea, I was desolate and bowed my head:
I have been faithful to thee, Cynara! in my fashion.

All night upon mine heart I felt her warm heart beat,
Night-long within mine arms in love and sleep she lay;
Surely the kisses of her bought red mouth were sweet;
10   But I was desolate and sick of an old passion,
When I awoke and found the dawn was gray:
I have been faithful to thee, Cynara! in my fashion.

I have forgot much, Cynara! gone with the wind,
Flung roses, roses riotously with the throng,
15   Dancing, to put thy pale, lost lilies out of mind;
But I was desolate and sick of an old passion,

> Yea, all the time, because the dance was long:
> I have been faithful to thee, Cynara! in my fashion.
>
> I cried for madder music and for stronger wine,
> 20   But when the feast is finished and the lamps expire,
> Then falls thy shadow, Cynara! the night is thine;
> And I am desolate and sick of an old passion,
> Yea, hungry for the lips of my desire:
> I have been faithful to thee, Cynara! in my fashion.

The poem is quite wonderful, isn't it?—in its fashion.

6.

A. R. Ammons, "Mansion" (1963)

We come, in closing, to a poem by the late A. R. Ammons—
Archie Ammons—who was a longtime professor here at Cornell,
and a major American poet.

You couldn't get farther from the conspicuous complexity and
artifice of Dowson's "Cynara" than the conspicuous simplicity and
artlessness of Ammons' "Mansion." Ammons renounces almost
all the traditional resources that mark the distinction between
poetry and ordinary speech. He gives up meter and rhyme for
free verse. He avoids the use of words and phrasing that, through
the nineteenth century and later, were the standard parlance of
poetry. How many noticed, for example, the number of poems
we have considered that said "thou," "thee," and "thy" instead of
"you" and "your"? "But how could I forget *thee*"; "waken *thou* with
me"; "I have been faithful to *thee*, Cynara." The use of that archaic
pronoun is an index to other locutions that we take for granted
in traditional poems, although written at a time when they were
rarely used in ordinary talk. In Ammons' "Mansion" we hear

instead a forthright, everyday American vernacular—with a slight North Carolina accent; the kind of plain talk that has no scruple about ending both of the first two sentences with a preposition: "to be delivered to"; "to show its motions with."

"Mansion" turns out to deal with a deeply human issue: What are we to make of life, knowing that we are mortal? But it begins with the utmost casualness—

So it came time / for me to cede myself—

as if death were the most natural thing in the world. (Ammons uses the word "cede" in the sense: "to officially turn myself over to.") The setting of the poem is the southwestern American desert, where the speaker addresses himself to the wind. So had many earlier poets. Shelley, for example, apostrophized the wind grandly—"O wild West Wind!"—at the beginning of his great "Ode to the West Wind." In "Mansion," however, the poetic speaker, with no rhetorical ceremony, engages the desert wind in a friendly chat. He offers his body to the wind—dust to dust—and by doing so, tacitly accepts his own participation in the natural cycle of life and death. (That's the rationale, in the fourth stanza, for the startling figure, "When the tree of my bones / rises from my skin"; the point is, that when he returns to dust, his sun-bleached rib cage will be as natural a part of the landscape as a desert tree.) For his offer the wind is grateful; because, it remarks, in playing its role in the natural cycle, it needs dust in order to make its motions visible. It then asks what it can do in return. In the lyric speaker's response, the colloquialism rises in stylistic pitch; the poet even introduces two quite unprosaic neologisms:

come and whirlwinding / stroll my dust. . . .

"Whirlwind" is a noun, but it is used here as the present participle of a verb. "Stroll" is an even bolder invention, because it is an intransitive verb used transitively—"stroll my dust." As such, it presses us to recognize that it is what Lewis Carroll's Humpty Dumpty called a portmanteau term; that is, it fuses the word "stroll" (to move casually) with the word "strew" ("strew my dust"). In "Mansion," however, this momentary heightening of the speech is whimsical; it serves only to remind us of the traditional high lyric style that this poem tacitly plays against, in order to achieve its distinctive countertraditional effects.

One last reference to the role of the fourth dimension—enunciation—in a poem. The word "whirlwinding" contains two prominent *w*'s. It is notable how often the speech-sound indicated by a *w* is foregrounded in other poetic references to the wind—in Shelley's "O wild west wind"; Shakespeare's "Blow, blow, thou winter wind"; A. E. Housman's

> The chestnut casts his flambeaux, and the flowers
> Stream from the hawthorn in the wind away. . . .

And for that matter, in Ammons' own very short wind-poem:

> The reeds give
> way to the
>
> wind and give
> the wind away.

That recurrent *w* is no accident. We form the speech-sound by compressing our lips and forcing air through them. That is, we blow the wind through our lips in the act of uttering poetic lines that signify the blowing wind: "whirlwinding."

The speaker, then, requests the obliging wind to blow his dust to a place where he can see the ocotillo (a cactus tree) and the desert wren. The phrasing is odd—deliberately odd, in order to suggest what it doesn't explicitly say. He asks the wind to strew his dust where

> I can see
>   how the ocotillo does
> And how saguaro-wren is. . . .

These phrases serve, tacitly, to humanize the relations of the lyric speaker to the ocotillo and the wren. They do so by echoing the two standard greetings between human beings—"How do you do?" and "How are you?"—but converting the second-person interrogative mode to the third-person declarative mode—"*how* do you *do*"; "*how* the ocotillo *does*"; "*how are* you?"; "*how* saguaro-wren *is*." In this way the tree and wren, like that other natural object the wind, are humanized, made companionable with the human observer, at the same time that all four are represented as fellow participants in the processes of nature.

In the last stanza, the speaker requests that, at nightfall, the wind drop his dust "here." I had read the poem a number of times before I recognized the significance of that simple locative adverb. The speaker asks that, after he dies, the wind deposit him here; that is, at the very place he is standing while he is talking to the wind, in order that, after death, he may continue to do—what? Exactly what he is doing at this place while alive.

Ammons' poem anticipating his mortality thus concludes in a tacit celebration of life, in such elemental enjoyments as looking at a desert tree, observing a desert wren, and finally, watching the dusk and anticipating the dawn. In its tone, furthermore, the closing segment of the poem also conveys, without saying so, an affirmation of life in this world. How does it manage this feat of communicating an essential point that it doesn't express?

For one thing, the speaker ends his request to the wind at

nightfall, yet looks forward to daybreak; the poem concludes—in a stanza that is one line shorter than the preceding stanzas—with the emphatic present tense of the verb, "breaks." And notice the slight surprise in the phrasing of the concluding line. Where we would expect the simple statement "and see the day break," we get instead "and think how morning breaks." "And *think*"; that is, he will ponder the possible significance of the fact that night gives way to day. By this phrasing, Ammons achieves also a subtle effect. At the end of the earlier stanzas of the poem, the free verse has tended to become metrical. Now, at the end of the entire poem, through all three of its closing lines, the irregular free-verse rhythms modulate into the assured, steady beat of an entirely regular iambic meter:

> whĕre wé căn wátch
> thĕ clósĭng úp ŏf dáy
> ănd thínk hŏw mórnĭng bréaks

Whatever Ammons may lose by not using a regular meter, he recuperates, in this and other poems, by resorting to that meter for special, unspoken purposes. By this and other means Ammons, without saying so, writes a poem about dying that celebrates the values in living. To put it the other way: The poet tacitly affirms life while tacitly acquiescing to the fact of his mortality.

I said earlier that the poem was conspicuously simple and art-less. The statement is, I think, true, but can be misleading. For in this, as in others of his lyric poems, in his individual—at times idiosyncratic—way, Ammons is a meticulous craftsman. It might be less misleading to put it this way: the effects of "Mansion" are produced by an art that hides its art, conspicuously. That is, Ammons intends his reader to be aware of what the poem does not say—of what it resists saying—and to be aware also of the standard artfulness of traditional poems in this lyric mode that this poem silently plays against.

An extreme instance of Ammons' reliance on what he doesn't tell you occurs at the very beginning of the poem, in the baffling title, "Mansion." What does a mansion have to do with the austere desert setting of this poem? The answer was provided to me by Roger Gilbert, my colleague at Cornell, who is writing what will be an indispensable book about Archie Ammons and his poetry: Roger showed me a statement Ammons wrote in 1987, in which he said that he was especially influenced as a poet "by the only poetry I knew as a child, hymns." To illustrate this influence, Ammons quoted the opening lines of a hymn. That hymn is called "An Empty Mansion," and Roger Gilbert found that it was included in a songbook that belonged to Archie's family. The first stanza (from which, remember, Archie quoted the opening lines in his listing of poetic influences), reads:

> Here I labor and toil as I look for a home,
> Just a humble abode among men,
> While in heaven a mansion is waiting for me
> And a gentle voice pleading "come in."

(The hymn is in turn a commentary on the biblical text of John 14:2: "In my father's house are many mansions.") There can be little doubt that, by naming it "Mansion," Ammons deliberately counterposes his poem against the purport of the hymn. That is: in choosing the wind to cede himself to, Ammons implicitly chooses, in preference to a mansion in the sky, what the hymn derogated as "just a humble abode"—an abode *here* amid the simplicities of the desert where, conjoined in a natural fellowship, and as fellow participant in the natural cycle of life and death, he can observe the ocotillo and the wren, watch the nightfall, and await the sunrise.

By relying throughout on indirection, suggestion, understate-

ment, and nonstatement, Ammons accepted the risk that his spare
and powerful little poem might slip by a casual reader as pleasant,
perhaps, but inconsequential. By the same token "Mansion" sets
anyone who undertakes to read it aloud with a daunting challenge:
How do you read what the poem says in such a way as to convey
the many other things, essential to the range and depth of its
meaning, that the poem, conspicuously, does not say?

MANSION

So it came time
    for me to cede myself
and I chose
the wind
5   to be delivered to

The wind was glad
    and said it needed all
the body
it could get
10   to show its motions with

and wanted to know
    willingly as I hoped it would
if it could do
something in return
15   to show its gratitude

When the tree of my bones
    rises from the skin I said
come and whirlwinding
stroll my dust
20   around the plain

so I can see
   how the ocotillo does
   and how saguaro-wren is
   and when you fall
25   with evening

   fall with me here
      where we can watch
      the closing up of day
      and think how morning breaks[3]

NOTES

Keats' Poems:
The Material Dimensions

THE CHIEF CONCERN of modern critics of Keats has been
with the semantic dimension of his poems—their component meanings; their thematic structures; and what, in
a well-known essay, Douglas Vincent Bush called "Keats and His
Ideas."[1] This was the primary issue for the New Critics of the mid-
century, who read Keats' poems with the predisposition to find
coherence, unity, and ironies; it is no less the issue for poststructural theorists, who read the poems with the predisposition to
find incoherence, ruptures, and aporias. The concern with seman-
tics is understandable, for Keats was a remarkably intelligent poet,
almost without parallel in the rapidity with which he grasped,
elaborated, and deployed philosophical and critical concepts. To

From *The Persistence of Poetry*, edited by Ronald M. Ryan and Ronald A.
Sharp (Amherst, Mass., 1998). This was a collection of papers delivered
at the John Keats Bicentennial Conference held at Harvard University
in September 1995. For additional analyses of the effects of the material
dimension of poems (the physical articulation of their speech-sounds), see
"The Fourth Dimension of a Poem," in this volume.

deal with his poems exclusively on the ideational level, however, is to disembody them and so to delete what is most characteristic about them. My aim in this essay is to put first things first: What is the immediate impact of reading a passage by Keats? And by what features do we identify the passage as distinctively Keatsian?

I

Consider the following lines from Keats' poems:

> My heart aches, and a drowsy numbness pains
> My sense, as though of hemlock I had drunk.

> From silken Samarcand to cedar'd Lebanon.
> Singest of summer in full-throated ease.

> whose strenuous tongue
> Can burst Joy's grape against his palate fine.

> Thy hair soft-lifted by the winnowing wind.

> 'Mid hushed, cool-rooted flowers, fragrant-eyed.[2]

The passages differ in what they signify, but we can say about all of them, as about hundreds of other lines, that if we were to meet them running wild in the deserts of Arabia, we would instantly cry out, "Keats!" On what features does this recognition depend?

Robert Frost used the word "sound" to describe the perceived aspect of a poem that is distinctive for each poet: "And the sound rises from the page, you know, a Wordsworthian sound, or a Keatsian sound, or a Shelleyan sound. . . . The various sounds that they make rise to you from the page."[3] The term is helpful, but it needs to be unpacked. In the current era of semiotics and

Derrida's warnings against "phonocentrism," we commonly refer to literary works as *"écriture"* and to poems as "texts." The material medium of poetry, however, is not the printed word. To think so is a fallacy—a post-Gutenberg fallacy of misplaced concreteness. Yet neither is the poetic medium a purely auditory sound as such. The material medium (in current parlance, "the material signifier") of a poem is speech, and speech consists of enunciated words, so that the sound of a poem is constituted by speech-sounds. And we don't—we can't—hear speech-sounds purely as sounds. Instead what we hear (to use Derrida's apt phrase) is "always already," and inseparably, invested with two non-auditory features. One of these is the significance of the words, phrases, and sentences into which the speech-sounds are conjoined. The other is the physical sensation of producing the speech-sounds that we hear or read. For when we read a poem slowly and with close attention, even if we read it silently to ourselves, the act involves—often below the level of distinct awareness—the feel of enunciating the words of the poem by remembered, imagined, or incipient movements and tactile sensations in the organs of speech, that is, in the lungs, throat, mouth, tongue, and lips. Because this feature, although essential to the full experience of a poem, has been neglected in literary criticism, I want to dwell for a while on the material, articulative aspect of Keats' language.

In taking pains, as Keats once said, to make a poem read "the more richly,"[4] he characteristically manages his language in such a way as to bring up to, or over, the verge of an attentive reader's consciousness what it is to form and enunciate the component speech-sounds. He makes us sense, for example, the changing size and shape of our mouth and the configuration of our lips as we articulate a vowel; the forceful expulsion of breath that we apprehend as syllabic stress; the vibration or stillness of our vocal cords in voiced or unvoiced consonants; the tactile difference between a continuant consonant and a stopped (or "plosive") consonant; and in the pronunciation of the various consonants, the movements of our lips and gestures of our tongue. Keats also makes us aware, as we pronounce consonants, of the touch of our tongue to the roof of the mouth or upper gum, and the touch of our lower lip to the teeth or (in labial consonants) of our lower lip on the upper lip. It is not possible to extricate with any precision the role of enunciation from those of sound and significance in the overall experience of a poem. It is evident, however, that Keats, by using long vowels, continuant consonants, and consecutive strong stresses to slow the pace at which we read, heightens our attention to the palpability of his material signifiers, and makes their articulation, juxtaposition, repetition, and variation into a richly sensuous oral activity. Consider the beginning of "Ode to a Nightingale":

> My heart aches, and a drowsy numbness pains
> My sense, as though of hemlock I had drunk.

In such passages, Keats enforces the realization that a poem, like other works of art, is a material as well as a significant thing; its significance is apprehended only by being bodied forth, and the poem's body is enunciated speech, which has a complex kinetic and tactile as well as auditory physicality. Of all the forms of art, furthermore, the material base of poetry, whether spoken or sung, is the most intimately human, because it is constituted solely by our own bodily actions, and because its vehicle is the breath of our life.

When discussing poems, we tend to attribute to the sound—the purely auditory qualities—of the words what are in much greater part the effects of enunciating the words conjointly with understanding the reference of the words. For example, in the line from "The Eve of St. Agnes,"

> From silken Samarcand to cedar'd Lebanon,

we say that the words are euphonious—that is, they sound good. But they sound good to the ear only because, meaning what they do, they feel good in the mouth; their pleasantness, as a result, is much more oral than auditory. It is a leisurely pleasure to negotiate the sequence of consonants in "cedar'd Lebanon": the oral move from *r* to *d* to *l*, concluding in the duplicated *n*'s, feels like honey on the tongue. And it is only because we articulate the phrase while understanding its references that we seem to hear in this line the susurrus of the silks from Samarcand.

All poets more or less consciously make use of the enunciative dimension of language, but Keats exceeds his predecessors, including his masters Spenser, Shakespeare (the Shakespeare of the sonnets), and Milton, in the degree and constancy with which he foregrounds the materiality of his phonic medium. In this aspect he also exceeds his successors, except perhaps Gerard Manley Hopkins, who stylized features he had found in Keats to stress the artifice of his coined compounds, repetitions and gradations of speech-sounds, and sequential strong stresses:

> Though worlds of wanwood leafmeal lie.[5]

Keats' awareness of the orality of his medium seems clearly connected to his sensitivity to the tactile and textural, as well as gustatory, qualities of what he ate or drank. For example, in a letter to his friend Charles Wentworth Dilke, he suddenly breaks off to say:

> Talking of Pleasure, this moment I was writing with one hand, and with the other holding to my Mouth a Nectarine—good god how fine—It went down soft pulpy, slushy, oozy—all its delicious embonpoint melted down my throat like a large, beatified Strawberry. I shall certainly breed. (*L*2:179)[6]

In our cultural moment of trickle-down Freudianism, Keats' orality of course invites charges of regression to the infantile stage of psychosexual development. Such speculations, I think, in no way derogate from his poetic achievement. A thing is what it is, and not another thing to which it may be theoretically reduced. Keats' remarkable sensible organization generated distinctive qualities of a great and original poetry, for which we need be grateful, whatever our opinion of its psychological genesis.

Keats' exploitation of the component features of a speech-utterance (oral shape, gesture, directionality, pace, and tactile sensations) helps account for another prominent aspect of his poetic language: its iconic quality. By "iconic" I mean the impression we often get, when reading Keats' poems, that his verbal medium is intrinsically appropriate to its referents, as though the material signifier shared an attribute with what it signifies. Alexander Pope, in a noted passage in *An Essay on Criticism*, said that in poetry "the sound must seem an echo to the sense."[7] As Pope's own examples show, this echoism is by no means limited to onomatopeia. Keats' iconicity is sometimes such a seeming mimicry of sound by sound: "The murmurous haunt of flies on summer eves" ("Ode to a Nightingale") and "The silver, snarling trumpets 'gan to chide" ("The Eve of St. Agnes"), for example. But sound mimicry is only one of many types of utterance mimicry in Keats. Take, as an instance, his notorious description, in his early poem *Endymion*, of what it feels like to kiss

Those lips, O slippery blisses.

Even after Christopher Ricks' acute and often convincing casuistry with respect to the morality and psychology of embarrassment in Keats' poetry,[8] many of us continue to find this line off-putting. This is not, I think, because Keats' phrase, in what Ricks aptly calls his "unmisgiving" way, signifies the moist physicality of an erotic kiss, but because the act of enunciating the line is too blatantly a simulation of the act it signifies, in the lip-smacking repetitions, amid sustained sibilants, of its double-labial stops. The blatancy is magnified by the effect of morpheme symbolism, that is, frequently recurrent combinations of speech-sounds in words that overlap in what they signify. In this instance, the iconicity of the *sl* combinations, heightened by the internal rhyme in "those lips" and "O slippery," is accentuated to the point of caricature by the underpresence of related sound-and-sense units such as "slither" and "slide," even, one must admit, "slobber" and "slurp."

But Keats is always Keatsian, and the oral gesture and sensation mimicry in his early and less successful passages remains the condition, subdued and controlled, of his later writing at its best. In the line "Singest of summer in full-throated ease" from "Ode to a Nightingale," the unhurried ease of articulating the open back vowels and the voiced liquid *r* and *l* in the spondaic "full-throated" is sensed, fully and deeply, within the resonant cavity of the throat to which the words refer. In Keats' description (in "Ode on Melancholy") of one

> whose strenuous tongue
> Can burst Joy's grape against his palate fine,

the plosive onset and muscular thrust of the tongue in uttering the heavily stressed "burst" duplicates the action of the tongue in crushing a grape, while, in enunciating the phrase "his palate fine," the touch of the blade of the tongue, in forming the consonants *l* and *n*, is felt on the palate that the words designate. In the line "as though of hemlock I had drunk" from "Ode to a Nightingale," to articulate the word "drunk" is to move with the vowel *u* from the frontal consonant *d* back and down through the mouth and throat, by way of the intermediate *r* and *n*, to close in the glottal stop *k*, in an act that simulates the act of swallowing that the word denotes. The effect is heightened by the anticipation of this oral gesture in the second syllable of "hemlock" and by its repetition in the following rhyme word, "sunk": "and Lethewards had sunk."

An instance that is subtler and more complex is Keats' description in "Ode to Autumn" of a personified Autumn sitting careless on a granary floor,

> Thy hair soft-lifted by the winnowing wind.

The exquisite aptness of this utterance to what it signifies is in part the effect of its changing pace and rhythm: the slow sequential stresses in "háir sóft-líftĕd" give way to fast-moving anapests— "sóft líftĕd bў thĕ wínnŏwĭng wínd"—in a way that accords with the desultory movement of the wind itself, as this is described in the next stanza of the poem. But the iconicity is to a greater degree the effect of the pressure and sensation of the inner airstream, the breath, that is sensed first in the throat in the aspirated (i.e., air-produced) *h* in "hair," then between the tongue and hard palate in the aspirated *s*, and on to the upper teeth and lower lip in the aspirated *f*'s of "soft-lifted," to become most tangible when the air is expelled through the tensed lips to form the *w* that occurs no fewer than three times—each time initiating the puff of air that forms the syllable *win*—in the two words that denote the outer airstream, "winnowing wind."

II

The conspicuous materiality of Keats' linguistic medium accords with the dense materiality of the world that his poems typically represent. In the line about bursting Joy's grape, for example, Keats converts an abstract psychological observation—only someone capable of the most intense joy can experience the deepest melancholy—into the specifics of eating a grape. And in this line from *Ode to Psyche*,

'Mid hushed, cool-rooted flowers, fragrant-eyed.

the references of the seven words, themselves so richly sensuous to utter, run the gamut of the senses of hearing, sight, odor, and touch (a touch involving both temperature and kinetic thrust in the spondaic compound "cool-rooted"). The materiality of Keats' representations, however, seems to run counter to his frequent practice, when referring to poetry in his letters, of applying to the imaginative process and its products such terms as "ethereal," "spirit," "spiritual," "empyreal," and "essence." In the traditional vocabulary of criticism, such terms have commonly been indicators of a Platonic philosophy of art, and this fact has led some commentators to claim that Keats—at least through the time when he wrote *Endymion*—was a Platonist in his theory about poetry, which he conceived as aspiring to transcend the material world of sense experience.

Platonic and Neoplatonic idealism is a philosophy of two worlds. One is the material world perceived by the human senses—a world of space, time, and contingency that is regarded as radically deficient because subject to change, loss, corruption, and mortality. To this the Platonist opposes a transcendent otherworld, accessible only to the spiritual vision. The otherworld is the locus of ultimate human desire because, since it consists of immaterial essences that are outside of time and space, it is unchanging, incorruptible, and eternal.

In an enlightening discovery, Stuart Sperry, followed by other scholars, showed that Keats imported "essence," "spirit," "spiritual," "ethereal," and related terms not from Platonizing literary theorists, but from a very different linguistic domain. In Keats' time, they were standard terms in a natural science, chemistry, in which Keats had taken two courses of lectures during his medical studies at Guy's Hospital in the years 1815 and 1816.[9] In the chemical experiments of the early nineteenth century, the terms were applied to various phenomena, and especially to the basic procedures of evaporation and distillation. When a substance was subjected to increasing degrees of heat (for which the technical term was "intensity"), it was said to be "etherealized," or refined; in this process, it released volatile substances called "spirits" and was purified into its "essences," or chemical components. The crucial fact, however, is that the products at the end of this process remain, no less than the substance at its beginning, entirely material things, except that they have been refined into what Keats called the "material sublime" ("To J. H. Reynolds, Esq."). ("Sublime" and "sublimation," as Sperry points out, were the terms for "a dry distillation.")[10] The technical vocabulary of chemistry, that is, provided for Keats' quick intelligence unprecedented metaphors for poetry—metaphors that made it possible to represent what he called the "silent Working" (*L*1:185) of the poet's imagination as a process of refining, purifying, etherealizing, spiritualizing, and essentializing the actual into the ideal without transcending the limits and conditions of the material world.

In the opening lines of his early poem *Endymion*, Keats says that he intended the work to be "A flowery band to bind us to the earth," that is, to this material world. When copying out the poem, Keats inserted the famed passage that he described, in a letter to his publisher, as setting out "the gradations of Happiness even like a kind of Pleasure Thermometer"; the writing of these lines, he added, "will perhaps be of the greatest Service to me of any thing I ever did" (*L*1:218). In these crucial but obscure lines, the gradations of happiness that culminate in what Keats calls "A fellowship with essence" have often been interpreted as a Platonic ascent to a supraterrestrial realm. Despite some coincidence of terminology, however, Keats' gradations are entirely opposed to the dematerializing process of philosophical meditation that Plato describes in the *Symposium*. In that dialogue, one climbs "as by a stair" from the beauty of a single material body up "to all fair forms," and then to "the beauty of the mind," in order to reach the goal of ultimate desire, the idea of "beauty, absolute, separate, simple, and everlasting." Keats' "Pleasure Thermometer," on the other hand (as the word "thermometer" implies) measures what he calls the "intensity" (the degree of heat applied to a retort in a chemical experiment)[11] in an imaginative ascent that is metaphorically equated with the stages of refinement in a process of evaporation and distillation. The ascent begins with the pleasurable sensations of physical things; these pleasures are successively refined and purified from all self-concern, until one achieves the selfless stage of "love and friendship." At the application of a final ("chief") degree of "intensity," the grosser (the "more ponderous and bulky") element of friendship is in turn separated out, leaving only, "full alchemiz'd," the purified "essence" that is love. Thus, at the end of the psychochemical procedure,

> at the tip-top,
> There hangs by unseen film, an orbéd drop
> Of light, and that is love.

As Donald Goellnicht acutely noted, this "orbéd drop" is "an exact description of a drop of pure distillate condensing on the lip of a retort to drip into a beaker."[12]

The point is important, because to Platonize Keats—just as to intellectualize or to textualize him—is to disembody him and thereby eliminate what is most Keatsian in his poems. To read him rightly, we need to recognize that he is preeminently a poet of one world, however painful his awareness of the shortcomings of that world when measured against the reach of human desire. And Keats' one world is the material world of this earth, this life, and this body—this sexual body with all its avidities and its full complement of the senses, internal as well as external, and what traditionally are called the "lower" no less than the "higher" senses. (Remember Keats' relish of a nectarine and of "Joy's grape.") His term for the goal of profoundest desire is "happiness," which he envisions as a plenitude of the physical and intellectual satisfactions in this earthly life, except that they have been purified from what he calls their "disagreeables." And in a "favorite Speculation," he imagines the possibility of enjoyments in a life "here after" as simply a repetition of "what we called happiness on Earth," except (this time Keats resorts to a musical instead of a chemical analogue) that it is "repeated in a finer tone and so repeated" (*L*1:185).

III

Lest I give the impression that I share the nineteenth-century view that Keats is a poet of sensations rather than of thoughts, I want to comment on the way that, at his mature best, he deals with matters of profound human concern but assimilates the conceptual import of his poems with the material qualities of his spoken language and the material particulars his language represents.

I concur with the readers for whom Keats' short ode "To Autumn" is his highest achievement. The poem is about a season of the year, but as in his other odes, the ostensible subject (a nightingale, a work of Grecian art, the goddess Melancholia) turns out to be the occasion for engaging with the multiple dilemmas of being human in the material world, in which nothing can stay. In "To Autumn," however, more completely than in the other odes, Keats leaves the concepts implicit in the choice and rendering of the things, events, and actions that the verbal medium bodies forth. My onetime teacher Douglas Vincent Bush was an acute, as well as learned, reader of poetry, but I think he was mistaken when he described Keats' "To Autumn" as "less a resolution of the perplexities of life and poetic ambition than an escape into the luxury of pure—though now sober—sensation."[13] On the contrary, Keats' poem is a creative triumph because, instead of explicitly treating a perplexity of life, he identifies and resolves a perplexity by incorporating it in a work that presents itself as nothing more than a poem of pure sensation.

A knowledgeable contemporary of Keats no doubt recognized what a modern reader is apt to miss, that "To Autumn" was composed in strict accord with an odd lyric model whose origins go back to classical times but which enjoyed a special vogue from the 1740s through Keats' own lifetime. This is the short ode (sometimes it was labeled a hymn) on a general or abstract topic. The topic is named in the title and formally invoked in the opening lines, where it is personified, given a bodily form, and accorded the status of a quasi divinity, usually female. The poem proceeds to praise, describe, and expatiate on the chosen subject, but it does this, strangely, in the grammatical mode of a second-person address to the personified topic itself. In this genre the direct precursors of Keats' "To Autumn" were the odes addressed to a time of year or a time of day, described by reference to scenes in nature; this subclass includes William Blake's short poems on each of the four seasons, written in the 1770s, in which Blake gives the standard matter and manner of the ode a prominently biblical cast and compacts them into the compass of sixteen to nineteen lines. Within this latter type, it seems to me likely that Keats' particular antecedent was William Collins' "Ode to Evening," published in 1746. But whether or not Keats remembered Collins while composing "To Autumn," it is useful to note the similarities between the two poems—in their use of the linguistic medium, their subject matter, and their poetic procedures—in order better to isolate what is distinctively Keatsian in this most formulaic of

Keats' odes and to identify the innovations by which he brought what was by his time a stale convention to vibrant life.

Collins' *Ode to Evening* is unrhymed; in place of the standard recurrences of terminal speech-sounds, his invocation exploits the enunciative changes in the procession of the speech-sounds inside the verse line:

> If aught of oaten stop, or pastoral song,
> May hope, chaste Eve, to soothe thy modest ear.

That is, Collins foregrounds the oral feel of producing the succession of vowels in the first line and of effecting the transition from the open back vowels (in "hope" and "soothe") to the closed front vowel (in "Eve" and "ear") in the second line.[14] He makes us all but aware, in enunciating these lines, that we produce the different vowels, even though the vibration of the larynx remains constant, by altering the configuration of our mouth and lips and by moving our tongue forward or back. He also brings to the edge of our awareness that the stopped consonants that punctuate these lines are effected by interrupting, with our tongue or lips, the sounding of the vowels: "If aught of oaten stop. . . ."

Collins goes on, always in the mode of an address to the personified evening, to detail selected scenes and events in the declining day, including prominently (as in "To Autumn") the sounds of insects. Later in the poem he holds constant the time of day and describes the change in a typical evening during each of the four seasons. By an inverse procedure, Keats holds the season constant and describes the changes during the course of a typical day, from the mists of the autumnal morning in the opening line to the setting of the sun in the closing stanza.

These and other parallels, however, only highlight the differences between the two poems. Collins' linguistic medium is only subduedly physical, and his descriptions are exclusively visual, intangible, and expressly represented as generic items in a conventional eighteenth-century landscape modeled on the paintings of Claude Lorraine. He asks to be led, for example,

> where some sheety lake
> Cheers the lone heath, or some time-hallow'd pile,
> Or up-land fallows grey
> Reflect its last cool gleam.

Keats, on the other hand, makes us feel, in the act of enunciating his words, the very weight, pressure, and fullness that he ascribes, not just to the physical processes by which autumn conspires (an interesting word!) with her "close bosom-friend," the virile sun, to "load," "bend," "fill," "swell," and "plump" the vines and trees, but also to their conspicuously edible products. Collins' Eve is young and virginal; she is "chaste," a "Maid compos'd," a "calm Vot'ress" from whom the male sun is segregated "in yon western tent." She is attended by an allegorical retinue of hours, elves, and "Pensive Pleasures sweet" but remains elusively diaphanous, emerging only to merge again into the visibilia of the landscape. "Be mine the hut" that

> marks o'er all
> Thy dewy fingers draw
> The gradual dusky veil.

But when Keats' autumn makes a personal appearance in his second stanza, it is as a mature woman who, far from dissolving into the outer scene, remains a full-bodied person who supervises, and sometimes herself engages in, the physical labors of the seasonal harvest.

This leads me to the important observation that whereas the setting of Collins' ode is the natural landscape, the setting of

Keats' ode is not nature but culture or, more precisely, the union of natural process and human labor that we call agriculture. Keats' poem was in fact inspired by the sight of a cultivated field just after it had been reaped. "Somehow a stubble plain looks warm," Keats wrote to his friend John Hamilton Reynolds. "This struck me so much in my sunday's walk that I composed upon it" (*L*2:167). In fact, in "Ode to Autumn," what Keats' descriptions denote or suggest allows us to reconstruct the concrete particulars of a working farm. Before us there is a cottage with a thatched roof around which grapevines have been trained. In the vicinity are the other plantings that provide what Keats calls the "store" of farm products—a grove of apple trees, a garden producing gourds and other vegetables, hazelnut trees, and a partly reaped grainfield. There are also a granary with a threshing floor, beehives, and on a near hillside a flock of sheep with their full-grown lambs.[15] In this Keatsian version of a georgic poem, two plants are mentioned that are not products of human cultivation, but both are explicity related to the activities of farming: the autumn flowers (9–11) that are harvested by the bees to fill the "clammy cells" of the farmer's beehive and the poppies (17–18) that are cut by the reaper in mowing the stalks of grain they entwine. In the first stanza, even the natural process of ripening is converted, figuratively, into a product of the joint labors of autumn and the sun, and in the second stanza, the four functions attributed to the personified Autumn all have to do with the workings of a cottage farm during the harvest: Autumn sits on the granary floor where the grain is winnowed; watches the oozings from the cider press; sleeps on a furrow that, tired by her labor, she has left only half-reaped; and carries on her head the basket of grain that has been gleaned in the cornfield.

Most important, finally, is the difference in the overall purport of the two poems. Collins' "Ode to Evening" is a fine period poem of the Age of Sensibility that is content to praise, with established odic ceremonial, the time and natural scenes favored by the lyric speaker, represented in the first person, who wanders through the poem as a typical penseroso figure and connoisseur of picturesque and sublime landscapes. He seeks out not only the "sheety lake" and "time-hallowed pile," but also, in stormy weather, the hut

> That from the mountain's side,
> Views wilds, and swelling floods,
> And hamlets brown, and dim-discover'd spires.

In Keats' "To Autumn," the lyric speaker never intrudes as a first-person participant or even by specifying his responses to what he describes. The descriptions, however, are represented not simply for their sensuous selves, but in such a way as to communicate what is never expressly said. Keats, that is, concretizes the conceptual dimension of his poem, which declares itself only by the cumulative suggestions of the phenomena he describes, the constructions of his syntax, the qualities and interrelations of the speech-sounds in which he couches his descriptions, and the increasingly insistent implications of the metaphors he applies to these phenomena in the course of the autumn day.

It is notable, for example, that "To Autumn" ends not in a decisive closure, but on a triple suspension—in syntax, meaning, and meter:

> And gathering swallows twitter in the skies.

The suspension is syntactic, in that the line (set off from what precedes it by a semicolon)[16] concludes a sentence that lists the varied contributors to the music of autumn, in which the only connective is a noncommittal *and*; Keats enumerates the sounds made by gnats *and* lambs, hedge crickets *and* redbreast; *and* gathering swallows . . . with which the series simply breaks off. The suspension is also semantic, in that "gathering," a present participle used adjectivally, signifies a continuing activity still to be completed.[17] Lastly, the suspension is metrical. The line can be read, according to the metric pattern established in the ode, with five iambic stresses:

And gáthering swállows twítter ín the skíes.

An expressive reading, however, does not stress the inconsequential preposition "in," but renders the line with only four strong stresses:

And gáthering swállows twítter in the skíes.

The result is that the poem closes with an empty fifth beat that we experience as portending something yet to come.

The multiple suspension, coming so unexpectedly at the conclusion to "Autumn," is inherently suggestive, and also heightens our retrospective awareness of earlier features of the poem. For example, there is the repeated use of present participles that indicate an ongoing, unfinished process, from "conspiring" in the third line to "gathering" in the last. We become more sensitive to the illusoriness of the bees' belief that "warm days will never cease" (10); to the emblematic associations, in stanza 2, with the scythe of a reaper only momentarily suspended; and to the portent in "the last oozings" of the cider press. The ending also sharpens our realization that in the last stanza the sunlit day of the preceding stanzas has lapsed into evening, and that although Autumn, as the lyric speaker reassures her, has her music, its mode, unlike that of "the songs of spring," is elegiac, in a tonality established by the gnats (27) who "mourn" in a "wailful choir" (the suggestion is of a church choir singing a requiem) even as the swallows are gathering for their imminent flight south.

We thus come to realize that the poem is from beginning to end steeped in the sense of process and temporality. Critics have often noted the static quality of Keats' descriptions, especially in the second stanza, but the seeming stasis, as the closing line both suggests and exemplifies, is in fact only a suspension on the reluctant verge of drastic change and loss. The precise moment of poise on the verge is denoted by the "now" in line 31. I must have read the poem a score of times before I realized the full poignancy of that word, coming at the end of a sequence of temporal adverbs beginning at line 25: "While," "Then," "and now" . . . the swallows are gathering. *Sunt lacrimae rerum.* What Keats expresses without saying, even as he celebrates the season of fruition, is awareness that in this world such fulfillment is only a phase in a process that goes on "hours by hours"; he expresses also his quiet acceptance of the necessity that this rich day must turn into night and this bountiful season into winter.

To return to the material base with which we began: Throughout the poem the interplay of the enunciated speech-sounds helps to effect—in fact, greatly enlarges—this conceptual reach beyond assertion. The final word of the last line, "skies," is itself experienced as a suspension, in that we need to go no less than four lines back for the word whose speech-sound, in the elaborate odic rhyme scheme, it replicates. That word is "dies"—

Or sinking as the light wind lives or dies.

Collins applies the same metaphor to the wind in his opening invocation to evening,

Like thy own solemn springs,
Thy springs and dying gales,

but "dying gales" was a stock phrase in the poetic diction of

Collins' time, and its function in his poem is simply to comport with the pervasive mood of "the Pensive Pleasures sweet." In Keats' "To Autumn," on the other hand, the wind that lives or dies resonates with a number of earlier elements in the poem; most markedly, it reiterates the metaphor in the phrase "the soft-dying day." These two allusions, reserved for the stanza that ends with the premonitory flocking of the swallows, widens the reach of reference from the processes of the natural world to the human speaker of the poem, for whom living and dying are not, as for the wind, the day, and the season, merely metaphors. The initial allusion to death, however, is oblique and is mitigated by its embodiment in a sequence of speech-sounds that are a delight to utter: "While barred cloúds blóom the sóft-dýing day." The procession is slowed for our closer apprehension by the two sets of successive strong stresses; as we enunciate the line, our awareness of the evolving changes in the seven long vowels (no vowel occurs twice) is enhanced by the slight impediments to be overcome in negotiating the junctures between adjacent consonants; while in the last two words the first syllable of "dying," by a vowel shift forward and up, modulates into "day," even as we realize that although the sunset can color ("bloom"), it cannot impede the death of the day.

Repetition cannot dull the sense of ever-renewing discovery in attending to the interrelations of material medium, metrical pace, syntax, tone of voice, and spoken and unspoken meanings in this marvelous stanza:

> Where are the songs of spring? Ay, where are they?
>   Think not of them, thou hast thy music too,—
> While barred clouds bloom the soft-dying day,
>   And touch the stubble-plains with rosy hue;
> Then in a wailful choir the small gnats mourn
>   Among the river sallows, borne aloft

Or sinking as the light wind lives or dies;
And full-grown lambs loud bleat from hilly bourn;
Hedge-crickets sing; and now with treble soft
The red-breast whistles from a garden-croft;
And gathering swallows twitter in the skies.

Since we are celebrating the two hundredth birthday of Keats, it seems appropriate to end this essay by situating his poem in the context of his life. "To Autumn" was the last work of artistic consequence that Keats completed. His letters and verses show that he achieved this celebratory poem, with its calm acquiescence to time, transience, and mortality, at a time when he was possessed by a premonition, little short of a conviction, that he had himself less than two years to live.[18] As it turned out, Keats died of tuberculosis only a year and five months after he composed his terminal ode. He was twenty-five years old. His career as a poet between his first successful poem, "On First Looking into Chapman's Homer," October 1816, and "To Autumn," September 1819, was limited to a span of thirty-five months.

NOTES

1. Douglas Vincent Bush, "Keats and His Ideas," *English Romantic Poets: Modern Essays in Criticism*, edited by M. H. Abrams (New York, 1960).
2. All quotations of Keats' poetry are from *The Poems of John Keats*, edited by Jack Stillinger (Cambridge, Mass., 1978).
3. Robert Frost, lecture on the bicentennial of Wordsworth's death (April 1950); transcribed from the tape recording in *The Cornell Library Journal* II (Spring 1970): 97–98.
4. *The Letters of John Keats: 1814–1821*, edited by Hyder E. Rollins (Cambridge, Mass., 1958), vol. 2, p. 106. Quotations of Keats' letters are from this edition, abbreviated *L* in the text; volume and page numbers are given in parentheses in the text.

5. Gerard Manley Hopkins, "Spring and Fall," in *Poems of Gerard Manley Hopkins*, edited by Robert Bridges and W. H. Gardner, 3d ed. (Oxford, 1948), p. 8.

6. I take "I shall certainly breed" to signify Keats' awareness that this kind of sense experience was effective in the poetry he composed.

7. Alexander Pope, "An Essay on Criticism," edition 2, line 365.

8. Christopher Ricks, *Keats and Embarrassment* (Oxford, 1974), pp. 104–5.

9. Stuart M. Sperry, *Keats the Poet* (Princeton, 1973), chap. 2. For a detailed treatment of Keats' medical training and its role in his poetry, see Donald C. Goellnicht, *The Poet-Physician: Keats and Medical Science* (Pittsburgh, 1984).

10. Sperry, *Keats the Poet*, p. 45.

11. Keats' use of "intensity" as the measure of the degree of heat in a process of evaporation is especially clear in his oft-quoted statement that "the excellence of every Art is its intensity, capable of making all disagreeables evaporate" (*L*1:192).

12. Donald C. Goellnicht, "Keats's Chemical Composition," in *Critical Essays on John Keats*, edited by Hermione de Almeida (Boston, 1990), p. 155.

13. Bush, "Keats and His Ideas," p. 337.

14. Collins' vowel play brings to mind Benjamin Bailey's testimony that one of Keats' "favorite topics of discourse was the principle of melody in Verse . . . particularly in the management of open and close vowels. . . . Keats's theory was that the vowels . . . should be interchanged, like differing notes of music to prevent monotony" (*The Keats Circle*, edited by Hyder E. Rollins [Cambridge, Mass., 1948], vol. 2, p. 277).

15. In Keats' draft of "To Autumn," a canceled line adds a barn to the cottage setting, after line 15: "While bright the Sun slants through the husky barn" (Stillinger, *The Poems of John Keats*, p. 477). The sacramental aura with which Keats invests the rich yields of the harvest season is suggestive of the rural scenes that Samuel Palmer was to paint some six years later, in the mid-1820s.

16. Although the punctuation varies in the various manuscripts of "To Autumn," the preceding line ends with a semicolon in the printed text of 1820, which Keats oversaw and for which he may have written out a printer's copy-manuscript. (For this matter, and for the

variations between "gathered" and "gathering swallows" below, I am indebted to Jack Stillinger's annotations in *The Poems of John Keats* and to his analysis of the facts in a letter to me dated May 19, 1997.)

17. In this passage Keats very probably recalled the lines in James Thomson's *Seasons:* "Warned of approaching Winter, gathered, play / The swallow-people. . . . They twitter cheerful" ("Autumn" [pp. 836–38, 846], see *The Poems of John Keats*, edited by Miriam Allott [London, 1970], pp. 654–55). Keats after some vacillation between "gathered" and "gathering," fixed on the latter form in the printing of 1820. It is notable that Thomson makes explicit the "approaching Winter," whereas Keats, although he names the spring, summer, and autumn, only implies the coming of the fourth season.

18. Aileen Ward, *John Keats: The Making of a Poet*, rev. ed. (New York, 1986), pp. 185, 431 n. 4; and 199–200, 432 n. 13b.

What Is a Humanistic Criticism?

Grau, theurer Freund, ist alle Theorie
Und grün des Lebens goldner Baum.
—Mephistopheles,
in Goethe's Faust, Part I

(Grey, dear friend, is all theory
And green the golden tree of life.)

I HAVE BEEN ASKED to present the opening paper for this symposium entitled "Critiquing Critical Theory." The term "theory" comprehends the innovative types of literary criticism, each based on a radical reconsideration of language and discourse, that since about 1960 have emerged in an accelerating sequence. The theories range from structuralism, through deconstruction and other poststructural schemes and interpretive

From *The Emperor Redressed: Critiquing Critical Theory*, edited by Dwight Eddins (Tuscaloosa, Ala., 1995). This was a paper presented at a symposium, "Critiquing Critical Theory," held at the University of Alabama in 1992.

practices, to some modes of the current New Historicism. And the term "critiquing" is used to signify a scrutiny by scholars and literary critics who have serious reservations about the assumptions and sweeping conclusion of these theories, at least in their extreme forms.

A critique is not a polemic. Many of the exchanges hitherto on these issues have been in a heated rhetoric of charges and counter-charges that clashes with the ideals of reasonableness and civility that one would like to profess in humane studies. I want instead to open this symposium with a brief overview of some recent critical theories in the spirit that John Stuart Mill, in his great essays comparing Bentham to Coleridge, attributed to Coleridge. Bentham asked of any doctrine "Is it true?" then judged it to be true only if it accorded with his prior opinions, and when it did not, attributed the doctrine to selfish interests or dubious purposes. My intention is to try, as Mill said of Coleridge, to look at some critical theories "from within," to ask what features and considerations have made them seem not only credible but compelling to intelligent and knowledgeable proponents, and to indicate the kinds of insights such theories have achieved that those of us who take an alternative intellectual stand would do well to heed. But I shall also indicate why, nonetheless, current theories, as applied in literary criticism, seem to me inadequate for the literature they undertake to explain and often distortive in the modes of reading they exemplify and recommend.

I. Opposing Paradigms of Language and Literature

Whatever their divergence, and their sometimes bitter internal quarrels, modern theorists coincide in a strenuous antihumanism and in discrediting or dismantling the interrelated concepts of "humanity," "human," "man," "the subject," "subjectivity," "the

person," and "the self." Claude Lévi-Strauss in fact redefined the
aim of the human sciences as the deletion of the human—"the
ultimate goal of the human sciences is not to constitute man
but to dissolve him"; and he and other radical structuralists represented the human subject as a product of systemic functions
and therefore, Eugenio Donato declared, "empty, uninhabited
by consciousness, emotion, affectivity, and so forth." As Roland
Barthes put it, "Don't I know that in the field of the subject,
there is no referent?" for "the subject is no more than an effect of
language." In his influential essay of 1970 announcing the decen-
tering of structuralism, Jacques Derrida described his deconstructive mode of interpretation, more guardedly, as one which "tries
to pass beyond man and humanism"; elsewhere he adverted to
his aim as "an entire deconstruction of onto-theological humanism (including that of Heidegger)." Earlier still, in *The Order of
Things* (1966), Michel Foucault, decrying "the chimeras of the
new humanism," announced in an oft-quoted passage that it is "a
source of profound relief to think that man is . . . a figure not yet
two centuries old, a new wrinkle in our knowledge, and that he
will disappear again as soon as that knowledge has discovered a
new form." And of what Foucault described as the "warped and
twisted forms of reflection" that even in this day wish to take
man "as their starting point in their attempts to reach the truth,"
he remarked contemptuously that "we can answer only with a
philosophical laugh."[1]

In much of our current cultural discourse, the effect of this
sustained onslaught has been to invert the emotional charge of
the terms "humanity" and "humanism" to a negative value and to
establish the presumption that any surviving humanist is someone who, out of nostalgia or timidity or self-interest, clings to
an exploded mythology. And some writers who adapt poststructural theory to a radical politics replace capitalism by humanism
as the root cause of social and political evils. A recent instance,

William Spanos' *The End of Education: Toward Posthumanism* (1993), charges humanism and its "commitment to the sovereign individual" with the major responsibility for the diverse forms of injustice and oppression, from imperialism and consumerism to the imposition of a core curriculum in liberal arts colleges.[2]

Current antihumanisms are usually underwritten by the claim that in Western thought and culture, appeals to the essential and universal nature of mankind have in fact served to empower, while masking, all modes of social, racial, and sexual repression. My concern is not with the validity of this historical claim about the normative and coercive uses of the term "human," except to note in passing that appeals to our common humanity have also served, historically, to ground the concepts of human rights and human values that enable antihumanists, no less than humanists, to identify the inequities and oppressions they oppose. Instead, my concern is to examine what an antihumanist stance comes down to, in the intellectual procedures of theorists who profess this point of view; and that is, the undertaking to dispense with any operative reference to human beings—conceived as purposeful agents capable of initiative, design, intention, and choice—in dealing with all linguistic utterances, discourses, and productions, including works of literature. How has this conceptual innovation been achieved?

The initiating move is a drastic change in the perspectival location, and the consequent frame of reference, for considering the use and products of language. From classical antiquity to the recent past, the reigning though often implicit locus for such theory had been that which in one form is exemplified here and now, where I as a speaker, standing in this room, address you as auditors. As a result, the traditional explanatory paradigm has been that of language-in-use: it posits language as the medium of a communicative transaction between human beings in a circumambient world. From this location and viewpoint, the understanding of a written product such as a work of literature is ultimately explicable by recourse to the same model as a spoken utterance—the model of a verbal transaction with a human being at each end; the difference is that the writing is usually done with the expectation of a reader rather than in the presence of an auditor, establishes a durable written correlate of a spoken utterance, and awaits the advent of a reader in order to complete the communicative transaction. Structural and poststructural theorists, on the other hand—and this is their novelty in the philosophy of language and literature—position their inquiry not in the human world of language-in-use, but in the abstract realm of language-in-general, or of discourse-as-such, or else in a text that is taken to exemplify such already constituted and intrasystemic workings of language or of discourse. Viewed from inside this paradigm, what had been the human agents in a verbal interchange are seen, and redescribed, as entities generated by the functioning of the language system itself, or else by the forces and configurations immanent in the discourse of a particular era.

Within the humanistic paradigm a work of literature, like any linguistic utterance or product, is conceived to be intermediary in a communicative transaction. Representative recent versions of this traditional conception of literature can be sketched, roughly, as follows: typically, an author initiates and composes a work that makes use of the resources afforded by the conventions and norms of a language to signify his or her intentional references to (for the most part fictive) people, actions, and states of affairs, in a way that will be intelligible to, and evoke responses from, a reader who shares a competence in the requisite linguistic conventions and norms.

What happens when the site of literary criticism is shifted from an interpersonal transaction to the process (in Paul de Man's phrase) of "language considered by and in itself"?[3] We find that the three traditional components of author, work, and reader survive, but in a severely attenuated state of being.

1. The author. Current theorists don't deny that a human individual is an indispensable factor in bringing about a literary product, but this is an author who, stripped of any design or intention that is effective in the product, is reduced to what Roland Barthes calls a "scriptor."[4] To radical structuralists, the author is merely a space in which the conventions, codes, and formal patternings of a *langue* precipitate into a *parole*. To radical poststructuralists, the author tends to become an agency through which the differential play of language-in-general instances itself in a text, or else (in Foucault and his followers) the author is a site or crossroad traversed by the constructs and configurations of power and knowledge that make up the discourse of an era. The traditional role of a supervisory and intentional "subject" is relegated to the status of a linguistic or discursive "function" or "effect." Jacques Derrida, for example, grants that "at a certain level" of experience and discourse, the subject as center "is absolutely indispensable"; but this is "a function, not a being—a reality, but a function." Or put otherwise: "There is no subject who is agent, author, and master of *différance*. . . . Subjectivity—like objectivity—is an effect of *différance*." And since "the names of authors . . . have here no substantial value" and "indicate neither identities nor causes," Derrida sometimes qualifies his "provisional" use of the name of an author by quotation marks, or else strikes a line through it, in order to identify whose (or rather what) text he is writing about while encoding the fact that he is not denoting a human author but indicating a textual effect.[5]

2. Radical theorists avoid using the traditional term "work" for a literary or other written entity, since the term suggests that the document has been accomplished by a purposive human producer. What had been a "work" is usually denominated a "text" or is still further depersonalized into an instance of *écriture*, writing-in-general. And in a literary or other text, what had traditionally

been its crucial aspect of referring to a world, whether actual or fictional, of persons, actions, things, and events is reconceived as a play of intratextual and intertextual significations. "What goes on in a narrative," Barthes wrote, "is, from the referential (real) point of view, strictly *nothing*. What does 'happen' is language per se, the adventure of language." And in default of any possible intervention by an author-subject, a text is in fact an intertext, "a tissue of quotations," a "multi-dimensional space in which a variety of writings, none of them original, blend and clash." Derrida recognizes in the reading of a text the occurrence of "effects" of "signification, or meaning, and of reference" as well as of other standard aspects of "semantic communication"; but from the standpoint of "a general writing," he says, this system of communication is revealed to be "only an effect, and should be analyzed as such."[6]

3. In the lack of an efficacious author or subject, one might expect that the reader would become the prime agent in effecting meaning; and indeed, some poststructural critics celebrate a reader's freedom in "creating" what a text is taken to signify. But it usually turns out that this reader is no more an effective, purposeful subject than is the author. Structuralist theory, as Jonathan Culler described it, "promotes analyses of the reader's role in producing meaning," but this is "the reader not as a person or a subjectivity but as a role: the embodiment of the codes that permit reading."[7] In poststructural theory, the human reader dwindles into *lecture*, an impersonal reading-process, or else, like the author, is evacuated into a textual effect. For a reader "to be fooled by a text," Barbara Johnson declares, "implies that the text is not constative but performative, and that the reader is in fact one of its effects."[8] And in theorists of various persuasions, the reader is represented in a doubly passive role, as constituted by, but also as the conduit of, the functionings of linguistic *différance*, or of the ideology and cultural formations in the reigning discourse,

or (in the theory of Stanley Fish) of the shared beliefs, categories, and reading process of a particular "interpretive community."

It should be noted that a traditional analyst of language recognizes that when a reader confronts a written or printed text, it is typically in the absence both of its author and of that to which a text refers; for the traditionalist, therefore, as well as for the poststructuralist, intentionality and reference are indubitably "effects" of the text. The difference is that poststructural theorists focus on language or discourse in being, in which all functions and effects are "always already" operative. To the traditionalist, however, a text's author-effect, intention-effect, reference-effect—and for that matter, its effect of being a set of signs instead of a mere sequence of blacks on blanks—are not attributable to the inner workings of a general writing, or of language as such, but have been constituted by the way human beings, in interpersonal dealings, have in fact learned to understand and to use language. In the view from the human paradigm, a text is cognizable as a set of verbal signs, and is invested with the effects of intentionality and reference that constitute its intelligibility, only to a reader who brings to the text foreknowledge, presuppositions, and skills acquired by prior experiences with the shared human practice of a language in a shared environing world.

This sharp disparity in the frame of theoretical reference comes clear in the noted controversy between John Searle and Jacques Derrida. To Searle, a meaningful sentence taken in isolation, in the absence of the writer, of the intended receiver, and of the context of its original production, is "just a standing possibility of the corresponding (intentional) speech act"—a possibility realized only if we apply to it our ordinary "strategy of understanding the sentence as an utterance of a man who once lived and had intentions like yourself."[9] Derrida, on the contrary, sets out from the general claim that "the total absence of the subject and object of a statement" is "structurally necessary"—that is, essential—to the functioning of any signifying system: "it is *required* by the general structure of signification, when considered *in itself.* It is radically requisite" to give "birth to meaning as such." And it is by adverting not to language-in-human-use but to "the general domain of writing"—in which the "radical absence" both of the writer and the receiver is "inscribed in the structure of the mark" and so "bound to the essential possibility of writing"—that Derrida draws the conclusion that "the system of speech, consciousness, meaning, presence, truth, etc. would be only an effect, and should be analyzed as such."[10]

Derrida not only takes his theoretical stand inside the domain of writing, or language in general, but stays there throughout his deconstructive analyses of the traditional concepts of communication. In discussing his much-quoted assertion of what he called "the axial proposition" of his *Grammatology, "Il n'y a rien hors du texte"*—"There is nothing outside the text"—Derrida has repeatedly stressed that the term "text," in his use, does not apply merely to printed pages but "embraces and does not exclude the world, reality, history," since these "always appear in an experience, hence in a movement of interpretation."[11] Derrida, that is, extrapolates the linguistic paradigm without limit so as to incorporate everything whatever into what he calls "a general writing," including the human participants and the environing world that are the constitutive elements in the humanistic paradigm. From Derrida's theoretical stance, all the world's a text, and the men and women who strive to read it are themselves texts, to themselves as well as to others; and as such, in the inevitable lack of a nontextual "pure presence" or "absolute presence" as an interpretive stopping place, all these have "never been anything but supplements, substitutive significations which could only come forth in a chain of differential references. . . . And thus to infinity."[12]

II. The Personification of the Text

A conspicuous feature in poststructural theories is that the initiative, signifying intentionality, and goal-directed purposiveness that have been subtracted from the traditional speaker or writer are not simply abolished, but are translocated into attributes of a personified text, or more generally, of a personified language-as-such. Barbara Johnson notes about Paul de Man that "even a cursory perusal of his essays reveals that their insistent rhetorical mode . . . is personification. In the absence of a personal agent of signification, the rhetorical entities themselves are constantly said to 'know,' to 'renounce,' or to 'resign themselves' in the place where the poet or critic as subject has disappeared." Johnson infers from this phenomenon that such predications do not signify attributes or actions of human agents that have been applied figuratively to language; instead, it indicates that personification is a floating figure per se, equally figurative whether applied to persons or things: "It implies that personification is a trope available for occupancy by either subjects or linguistic entities, the difference between them being ultimately indeterminable, if each is known only in and through a text."[13]

Examination reveals that an insistent prosopopeia of the text is not limited to de Man but is so ubiquitous in deconstructive writings—including those of Barbara Johnson—as to make it a prime identifier of the deconstructive style. In fact, personification seems indispensable to a stance within textuality that, denying an effective role to human enterprise, needs to posit an immanent cunning of *différance* in order to set a text into motion and to generate its significative and other "effects," as well as to provide some semblance of directionality to what Derrida calls its "play" and its "working." Typical is the reiterated assertion that a deconstructive reading is not something that a reader does to a text, but a replication of something that the text has always already done to itself. As Derrida puts this claim: "Deconstruction is not even an *act* or an *operation*. . . . Deconstruction takes place, it is an event that does not await the deliberation, consciousness or organization of a subject. . . . *It deconstructs it-self. It can be deconstructed. [Ça se déconstruit.]*"[14]

Attributions of human powers and actions to a text, or else to discourse, are frequent also in other poststructural modes. "It is the text," Barthes says, "which works untiringly, not the artist or the consumer"; and, in an echo of Heidegger's *"Die Sprache spricht, nicht der Mensch,"*: "It is language which speaks, not the author."[15] In the writings of Foucault, it is a disembodied "power," operating in the social entity and its discourse, that is invested with motility, aims, and productivity. Power, as he says, "traverses and produces things, it induces pleasure, forms knowledge, produces discourse." "Power must be analysed as something which circulates"; the human individual does not exert power but is himself "an effect of power," who is "constituted" by power and "at the same time its vehicle."[16] In other types of current theory, a goal-directed enterprise and the production of meaning and effects are attributed to the secret workings, within texts and discourse, of "ideology," or to an unpersoned agency called "history"—a history, as Stephen Greenblatt epitomizes the assumption of the New Historicism, that is not something external to texts but "is found in the artworks themselves, as enabling condition, shaping force, forger of meaning, censor, community of patronage and reception."[17]

A number of other textual tropes give a distinctive quality to deconstructive and other poststructural writings. Especially pervasive are the figures of violence and murderous conflict that, to the startled traditional reader, make the field of language and discourse seem a killing field. "We must conceive discourse," Foucault declares, "as a violence that we do to things"; and he decries the static peacefulness of the structural model for semiology:

> One's point of reference should not be to the great model of language [*langue*] and signs, but to that of war and battle. The history which bears and determines us has the form of a war rather than that of a language. . . . "Semiology" is a way of avoiding its violent, bloody, and lethal character by reducing it to the calm Platonic form of language and dialogue.[18]

In Derrida's formulations, language is structured by violences throughout. The very fact of naming "is the originary violence of language," revealing that self-presence is "always already split," while proper names implicate death, since by their capacity for surviving those that they designate, they inscribe the possibility of their death. In discussing what he claims is "the anxiety with which Rousseau acknowledges the lethal quality of all writing," Paul de Man explains that "writing always includes the moment of dispossession in favor of the arbitrary power play of the signifier and from the point of view of the subject, this can only be experienced as a dismemberment, a beheading or a castration."[19]

Especially in deconstructive writings, a common model for intertextual conflict is that of an *agon*, a struggle for mastery between diverse opponents. One of the antagonists may be the intention, as Derrida puts it, of "the presumed subject," which is always doomed to fail in the attempt to "dominate," or "command," or "master" the forces internal to the language of a text. Or it may be the struggle of a reader to understand a text's meaning; but this endeavor, Hillis Miller says, merely "forces [the reader] to repeat in his own way an effort of understanding that the text expresses, and to repeat also the baffling of that effort."[20] For the most part, however, deconstructive critics represent both antagonists as inhabitants of the text itself. Paul de Man posits an omnipresent contestation between the regular and the unruly aspects of a text, which he denominates as the constative and cognitive against the performative, or else as the grammatical and logical against the rhetorical, or the aspect of rhetoric as persuasion against the aspect of rhetoric "as a system of tropes." In each of these modes, the result is an aporia between "two incompatible, mutually self-destructive points of view" that puts "an insurmountable obstacle in the way of a reading or understanding." In the best-known thumbnail definition of deconstructive criticism, Barbara Johnson formulates it as "the careful teasing out of warring forces of signification within the text itself," in which there is no "unequivocal domination of one mode of signifying over the other."[21] That is, the antagonistic forces inhabiting a text remain forever locked in the "double-bind" or "aporia" or "abyme" of opposed but unresolvable significations that an all-out deconstructive critic finds in reading any and all works of literature, or, for that matter, in reading any writing whatever.

III. The Death and Life of the Author: Barthes, Foucault, and Horace

The most widely known representations of the literary text as inherently and autonomously active are the essays by Barthes and Foucault which announce, with Nietzschean melodrama, that the author is dead.[22] The demise is not, of course, of the scriptor of a text but of what these theorists describe as a recent social construct, or "figure," that performs what Foucault calls the "author function." In literary criticism, it is claimed, the author figure has served not only to classify and interrelate texts under an authorial proper name but also to establish a literary discourse as a property—in Foucault's terms, as "a product, a thing, a kind of goods"—of which an author is the owner; to ascribe meaning, status, and value to a literary text according to the author to whom it is assigned; to attribute the origins of a text to a "motive" or a "design" in the author construct; and to "explain" it as an expression of that author's "life, his tastes, his passions." Both writers agree, furthermore, that the cardinal function of the modern author figure has been to enforce a limit on the free generation of meanings by a literary text. Since the eighteenth century, Foucault says, the "functional principle" of an author "allows a limitation of the cancerous and dangerous proliferation of significations. . . . The author is the principle of thrift in the proliferation of meaning."[23] Roland Barthes hails the emancipation of textual meanings that has now been achieved by the death of the author on whom, he asserts, "the image of literature . . . is tyrannically centered":

> To give a text an Author is to impose a limit on that text, to furnish it with a final signified, to close the writing. . . . [But] literature (it would be better from now on to say writing), by refusing to assign a "secret," an ultimate meaning, to the text (and to the world as text), liberates . . . an activity that is truly revolutionary since, to refuse to fix meaning is, in the end, to refuse God and his hypostases—reason, science, law.[24]

Several commentators have remarked that Barthes and Foucault wrote their essays in 1968 and 1969 and that they apply to literary texts the perfervid liberation rhetoric of the student uprisings in Paris of May 1968. But whatever the conditions of their production, these essays are often reprinted and have achieved something close to canonical status among poststructural writings. It is worth pausing, therefore, to ask, How accurate, as history, are the stories that Barthes and Foucault tell about the time and the social causes of the emergence, in standard discourse about literature, of the author figure and author functions they describe?

Both writers assign what Foucault calls "the coming into being of the notion of 'author,'" with respect to literature, to the era between the late seventeenth and early nineteenth centuries; and they agree that the developed author functions are products of the bourgeois ideology engendered by a capitalist economy. The "positivism," according to Barthes, "which has attached the greatest importance to the 'person' of the author" is "the epitome and culmination of capitalist ideology"; while to Foucault, the author as textual proprietor and "regulator of the fictive" is "an ideological product" that is "characteristic of our era of industrial and bourgeois society, of individualism and private property."[25] The question suggests itself: How, then, were an author and his functions conceived during the many centuries of written literature before the development of capitalism and its bourgeois ideology—as far back, for example, as classical antiquity? We might glance at Horace's *Ars Poetica*, because, although written in verse, its mode of informal advice to a would-be poet is more likely to represent then current discourse about poetry than the more formal or technical writings by Aristotle and other Greek and Roman inquirers.

We find that Horace takes for granted a situation in which poetic works are grouped and interrelated by assignment to individual authors—he names a range from Homer to his contemporary Virgil—who as composers of their works are responsible for their subject matter, form, and quality, whether to their fame or to their discredit. A good *poeta*, or "maker"—Horace in his epistle also refers to the poet as *auctor* and *scriptor*—must possess native talent (*ingenium*) but must also train himself to become a master both of language and of the poetic art. The competent poet deliberately designs and orders his *poema*, adopts and adapts his words, and selects and renders his materials in order to evoke, by their understanding of what he writes, the emotions of his audience or readers, as well as to achieve for them *utile* and *dulce*, profit and delight. To the dramatic poet Horace recommends, after he has become "a trained imitator [*doctum imitatorem*]," that he should look to "life and manners as the model from which to draw talk that is true to life [*vivas . . . voces*]" (lines 317–18). As a consequence his poem will depict credible and consistent persons such as are familiar to its readers—persons who must themselves express feelings if they are to evoke those feelings: *"Si vis me flere, dolendum est / primum ipsi tibi"* (lines 102–3).

What of the function that would seem most plausibly specific to authorship under capitalism—that which invests an author with proprietorship of a text that is sold for profit? According to Foucault, the conception of a literary text as "a kind of goods" that is "caught up in a circuit of ownership" developed "once a system of ownership for texts came into being . . . at the end of the eighteenth and beginning of the nineteenth century."[26] But some two thousand years before that, Horace had declared that a poetic book that both instructs and delights the reader (lines 343–45) will not only be posted overseas and prolong the author's fame; it will also "earn money for the Sosii," the famed Roman booksellers.[27] We know from sources besides Horace that, even in an era when texts were published in papyrus rolls that were copied by hand, there was a flourishing trade in the making, selling, and exporting of books for profit.[28] Horace also warns us (lines 372–73) that "for poets to be mediocre has never been tolerated—not by men, or gods, or *columnae*." *Columnae* is usually translated simply as "booksellers"; but it in fact denoted the columns or pillars outside a bookseller's establishment on which he advertised his wares. Clearly, Horace conceived and discussed books of poetry as commodities advertised for profitable sale, in which the author had not only a personal involvement as his individual accomplishment but a proprietary interest as well.

It seems, then, that whatever the differences in economic and legal circumstances and in conceptual nuances, the figure and functions of a literary author in the cultivated discourse of Horace's time were pretty much what they are now, at least in non-poststructural discussions. More generally, and more important, Horace clearly takes for granted a version of the humanistic paradigm—a version in which a purposive author designs and effects a poetic work that represents, or "imitates," credible human beings and actions and is addressed to the understanding and the emotional and pleasurable responsiveness of human readers. And if we look further, we find this paradigm, as well as similar conceptions of the role of a literary author, in Aristotle's *Poetics*, in Longinus on the sublime style, and in the classical writers on rhetoric.

Afterward, this overall frame of reference for critical treatments of poetry, and of literature in general, remained in place for some two millennia. The large-scale changes that occurred in the long history of literary criticism can be mapped mainly in terms of an altering focus on one or another of the elements within this frame, as the emphasis shifted between the makeup of the environing world; the needs and preferences of readers; the temperament, imagination, and emotional processes of the author; and the internal requirements of the work itself as the primary (although almost never exclusive) determinant in making a literary work what it is.[29] The human world of language-in-use thus served as a locus and paradigmatic frame for almost all general discourse about literature until three or four decades ago, when it was displaced by the theory worlds of structural and poststructural criticism.

IV. Human World and Theory Worlds

The traditional paradigm for considering language and literature presumes a shared world in which human beings live, act, and converse and in which, if they are philosophers, they then go on to formulate theories about that world. In the Platonic dialogues such is the world, with its solid physical settings and lively interpersonal exchanges, in which Socrates proceeds to set forth the theory that this world is merely appearance when measured against the criterion world of Reality. Such also is the world described by Descartes in which, "sitting by the fire, clothed in a winter robe," he manipulates a lump of beeswax and observed through the window "human beings going by in the street," while excogitating the possibility of doubting the reality of that world and of everything in it except that he is doubting.[30] And it is the world into which, David Hume tells us, the unreasoning force he calls "nature" redelivers him after he has reasoned himself into denying any justification for believing the reality of an outer world, of human beings, and even of his "personal identity" or "self." From the "forlorn solitude" of his skeptical theory world, Hume says, he returns to the world where "I dine, I play a game of backgammon, I converse, and am merry with my friends"—a human world, that is, in which "I find myself absolutely and necessarily determin'd to live, and talk, and act like other people in the common affairs of life"; although only until he again isolates himself in order to recommence his theoretical speculatings "in my chamber, or in a solitary walk by a river-side."[31]

Some version of such a world, within which people purposefully act, interact, and communicate, has been the primary site assumed by British and American philosophers of language in the recent past, whether they are analytic philosophers or ordinary language philosophers or write in the tradition of American pragmatism. In Ludwig Wittgenstein's later thinking, a special concern, within what he sometimes calls our *Weltbild*, is with the primitives, the "givens" which, when we set out to justify our beliefs and assertions, turn out to be end points—the "bedrock," as he puts it, where "my spade is turned." And at such termini of the "chain of reasons," he famously declares, "what has to be accepted, the given is—so one could say—*forms of life*." Such givens in our "world-picture," the "substratum of all my enquiring and asserting," Wittgenstein points out, do not consist of self-evident, asserted truths, or of quasi-visible presences, but of participation in ongoing, shared human practices. "Giving grounds . . . justifying the evidence, comes to an end;—but the end is not certain propositions striking us immediately as true, i.e., it is not a kind of *seeing* on our part, it is our *acting*, which lies at the bottom of the language-game."[32] It might be said, then, that we enact our primitive certainties in the conduct of our lives and of the language that is interinvolved with the ways we live. And among the givens in our lived world are human beings, in whom we spontaneously recognize an I in the other and manifest that affinity in the distinctive ways we feel toward them and with them, and deal with them, and talk to and about them. Such certainties that "stand fast" for us are not empirical assertions capable of proof, but they do not need to be proved, for they function not only as the presuppositions of all proofs but also as the preconditions without which it is not possible to account for the historical development of a common language and for the fact that each of us learns to use and understand a common language.[33]

To the outlook of a humanistic criticism, such givens are constituents of the world in which we live and move and have our meanings. It is a human world not only in that it contains human beings but also in that it is always and only a world-for-us, given our human senses, physiology, and prior history; what it would be if (in Keats' phrase) we could "see as a God sees"[34] is beyond conjecture. And from the earliest records to the present, such a world has been represented in literature, in which persons recognizably (however distantly) like ourselves perceive, talk, think, feel, and enact a story within a recognizable version (however altered) of the human world we live in; even the authors of Mallarméan, or surrealist, or magical realist, or other works that set out to escape the conditions of our world cannot but rely for their effects of unreality on violating the presuppositions formed by our experiences in that world. Finally, such a world also constitutes the site, or tacit frame of reference, common to traditional critics of literature, including many philosophers who, in their theories about the world, are idealists or skeptics rather than realists—when, that is, they write not as metaphysicians but as critics of specific works of literature.[35]

Now, what do the distinctive themes and enterprises of radical structural and poststructural theorists look like from the viewpoint of someone positioned, philosophically, within this human world?

One would have to read the major innovative theorists in what Jonathan Swift sardonically called "the true spirit of controversy"—that is, "fully predetermined against all conviction"—not to find a great deal that is profitable and enlightening in what these theorists have to say. A useful way to clarify the nature of their contributions, I think, is to apply to them three criteria that can be disengaged from an early essay by Derrida himself, "Force and Signification" (1963), in which he assayed the achievements, but also the limitations, of structuralism as applied in literary criticism.[36]

1. First, Derrida attributes to "the structuralist invasion" what he calls "an adventure of vision, a conversion of the way of putting questions to any object." Applying this criterion, one can say that certainly, by a radical shift of perspective, poststructuralists as well as structuralists have defamiliarized, and so impelled a reexamination of, what one tends to take for granted; not least by the drastic conversion that turns the human world outside-in, asking us to try the adventure of envisioning human subjects not as the agents but as the functions or effects of texts or discourses.

2. Derrida specifies a second use of a theory as an "operative concept," or "a heuristic instrument, a method of reading." It seems obvious that, when employed as a heuristic instrument, or discovery-procedure, each major theory, in part by virtue of the exclusivity of its focus, has effected insights that advance our understanding. What dispassionate inquirer would deny the profit in the structuralist's distinctive inquiry into the degree to which a literary work manifests the repetition, variation, and internal relationships of preexisting structures, formulas, and codes? Or the kinds of discoveries made possible by Foucault's innovative approach to the human sciences, not in order to determine whether their predications are true to the way things really are, but in order to investigate the discursive "*régime* of truth" in which the predications play their role—that is, to inquire into the historical conditions that have engendered the forms of discourse in which such predications are *accounted* to be true. Or the value of Derrida's examination of the ways that what we say and think are conditioned by the material and formal features of our language and structured by the deployment of tacitly hierarchical oppositions; and also of his expositions of the ineluctable role that metaphors play in philosophical discourse, especially the figure of visibility, light, and darkness which, he says, is "the founding metaphor of Western philosophy as metaphysics."[37]

3. But Derrida also identifies an aberrant application of structuralism when, no longer simply a heuristic instrument for investigating a literary object, "structure becomes the object itself, the literary thing itself . . . the exclusive *term* . . . of critical description." In such instances structure becomes "in fact and despite his theoretical intention the critic's sole preoccupation" and so "the very being of the work." Derrida's objection to what he calls this "ultrastructuralism," as I read him, is that it transforms a useful perspective into an exclusive doctrine and a heuristic

position into an objective imposition. I want to pose the question: Can this charge be leveled also against some widespread uses of poststructural theories? And first, does it apply to Derrida's own deconstructive procedures, "in despite," as he said about ultrastructuralism, of the proponent's own "theoretical intention"?

The answer depends on where you read Derrida and on how you read his elaborately allusive and elusive prose. He insists that by "deconstructing" or "dismantling" the concepts and structures of our logocentric language, he does not "destroy" or "discard" them but simply "situates," "reinscribes," or "reconstitutes" them in alternative contexts; and he stresses that deconstruction does not and cannot propound a science of language, or a counterphilosophy to Western philosophy, or an alternative order to that of logocentric truth.[38] In such passages, it seems clear, deconstruction is proffered as a tactic to uncover, redescribe, and put to question, but without either the intention or the possibility of destroying, or supplanting, the procedures of our ordinary linguistic practices. As Barbara Johnson describes it, a deconstructive reading "does not aim to eliminate or dismiss texts or values, but rather to see them in a more complex, more *constructed*, less idealized light."[39]

Richard Rorty, assimilating Derrida's deconstructive intent to his own neopragmatism, has praised Derrida as the inventor of "a new splendidly ironic way of writing about the philosophical tradition"—that is, as providing a novel point of vantage from which to view all philosophies with skeptical irony. But Rorty goes on to ask, Is Derrida in addition a "transcendental philosopher" who sets forth a new and better philosophy of his own? and then acknowledges that Derrida indeed "makes noise of both sorts."[40] To me, Derrida sounds most like a deductive type of transcendental philosopher when, from his theoretical position within the functioning of language-in-general, he posits a prelinguistic and preconceptual nonentity that he calls a "mark" or "trace," ascribes to it such "structural" (that is, essential) features as *différance* and iterability (repeatability, hence an inescapable difference from itself, or "alterity"), and then draws consequences that necessarily obtain not only for our practice of language and of all other signifying systems but also for "the totality of what one can call experience." Derrida asserts, for example: "The graphics of iterability inscribes alteration irreducibly in repetition (or in identification): a priori, always and already." This iterability, he says, is "the very factor that will permit the mark . . . to function beyond this moment," but by that very possibility it also "breaches, divides, expropriates the 'ideal' plenitude or self-presence of intention, of meaning (to say)"; it thus "leaves us no choice but to mean (to say) something that is (already, always, also) other than what we mean (to say), to say something other than what we say *and* would have wanted to say, to understand something other than . . . etc."[41] Such reasoning would seem to ensure that, in our actual practice of using and understanding language—and of experiencing the world—we cannot but find the features that we have inserted, "a priori, always and already," into our theoretical premises.

An inquirer, on the other hand, whose stand is in the world of human relations and interactions, takes language to be a very complex set of shared social practices and, upon investigating those practices, finds that we often manage very well to say what we mean and to understand what someone else has undertaken to say. Such an inquirer—John Austin, for example, about whose views Derrida wrote a deconstructive critique that set off his controversy with John Searle—identifies clear cases of successful speech-acts in our practice of language, and then sets out to explain how that practice works by specifying conditions that, when they are satisfied, will serve to account for our communicative successes and that, when they are not satisfied, will serve to account for our communicative failures. Such an inquirer does this in the recognition that no case of communicative success is an absolutely clear case, in that one can never be absolutely certain that all the conditions necessary for success have been fully satisfied; such infallible judgments require access to a self-warranting warrantor of certainty—whether we call it an absolute, or presence, or transcendental signified, or onto-teleological entity—forever outside the reach of human finitude. To the empirical inquirer into our practice of language, the index of success in communication is more modest than absolute certainty; it is practical certainty, an adequate assurance that we have understood each other, given the kind of language game in which we happen to be engaged and the circumstances of the particular utterance. It remains always and unavoidably possible, however, that we have got the thing wrong, although that possibility may be extremely slight in this or that instance of linguistic interchange.

What on the contrary distinguishes a radical, or strong, poststructuralist is that he or she sets out from a theoretical predetermination of the necessary nature of language as such, or of discourse in general, and reasoning *von oben herunter*, evolves conclusions about what our linguistic and discursive practices and experiences must necessarily be. And when the ways we in fact use language don't jibe with these theoretical conclusions, the strong theorist privileges the conclusions to overrule our practices and experiences, which are discredited, or at any rate drastically derogated, as no more than effects, functions, illusions, false consciousness, or mystifications. However one reads the puzzling deliverances on the issue by Derrida himself, this is the typical way of proceeding of all-out practitioners of deconstructive literary criticism. It is also the procedure of the radical Foucauldians who reason down from the universal premise that all discourse, hence all thought and knowledge, consists of cultural constructs effected and directed by the forms and circulation of power; or of the poststructural Marxists who reason down from the premise that all discourse is constituted by an ideology in the secret service of class interests or a controlling elite; or of that special group of poststructural feminists who reason down from the premise that all Western discourse is inherently and in totality phallocentric, thereby disqualifying a priori all possible counterclaims (and for that matter their own claims) as necessarily and irredeemably sexist. In this way a theoretical position that may have value as an adventure in vision, or as a speculative instrument for discovery, suffers a hardening of the categories and becomes a Grand Theory. Or to put the matter in a different figure: a tentative working hypothesis becomes a tyrannical ruling hypothesis whose consequences are projected as the way things really are, because by logical necessity they must be so. In such extreme instances the result is that the human world in which people deploy language in their diverse purposes, for good and for ill, is displaced by a theory world in which people are not agents but agencies, not users of language but used by language, not effectors but themselves only effects.

V. *The Alien Vision*

I don't have confidence that the divergence between a confirmed humanist and a confirmed poststructuralist stands much chance of being overcome by rational argument; in each instance, the initiating position, or founding intuition, is too thoroughly implicated in an overall outlook to be vulnerable to counterreasoning from an alternative outlook. The deep-rooted and ever-reviving disputes that make up the history of philosophy indicate that there is no knock-down, drag-out argument that will dislodge a proponent from an initiating position; he can be dislodged only by a philosophical conversion experience—"a conversion," as Ludwig Wittgenstein, who had himself undergone such an experience, described it, "of a special kind," in which one is "brought to look at the world in a different way."[42] But recognition of this circumstance has never stopped philosophers from arguing against counterphilosophies; nor will it stop me from concluding this talk with a couple of arguments—more properly, a couple of considerations—that bear against inhumanist modes of poststructural criticism; realizing that these will seem convincing only to those who already occupy the humanistic position, yet with the faint hope that someone out there is listening who may be susceptible to a perspectival conversion.

My first consideration is exemplified in the response of the young Goethe when he read the Baron d'Holbach's *System of Nature* (1770); this was an early and ably reasoned form of postscientific inhumanism, in which d'Holbach, arguing against religious supernaturalism, undertook to undo human consciousness, purposiveness, and initiative as philosophical primitives by reducing them to the material operation of causal laws. This book, Goethe wrote, "appeared to us so dark, so Cimmerian, so deathlike, that we found it difficult to endure its presence, and shuddered at it as at a specter. . . . How hollow and empty did we feel in this melancholy, atheistical half-night, in which earth vanished with all its images, heaven with all its stars."[43] Note that Goethe's response is not an argument addressed against d'Holbach's arguments but an expression of incredulity toward the world that is the consequence of d'Holbach's arguments—a world that Goethe finds to be unreal, and also morally repulsive. And then there is Samuel Johnson's response to Boswell's challenge that it is "impossible to refute" Bishop Berkeley's claim that "every thing in the universe is merely ideal." Johnson's reply is not an argument but a gesture—"striking his foot with mighty force against a large stone, till he rebounded from it, 'I refute it thus.'"[44] It is common to say that Johnson's response is naïve, but anyone who has read Johnson's essays knows that he is not in the least philosophically naïve. The stone that Johnson kicks is an object out there in the human world, and the gesture tacitly declares that he finds Berkeley's theoretical stone, existing only as a collection of ideas in minds, to be humanly unbelievable; perhaps with the further implication that if one's reasoning leads to unbelievable consequences, it would be reasonable to reconsider the epistemological premises that result in these consequences.

In a parallel way, traditional readers find the theory world of all-out poststructural critics to be a blatant mismatch to the world in which we live, write, and read works of literature, and also to the world we find represented in the works we read. For in reading literature, we, like the myriads of recorded readers before us, commonly discover characters who, although fictive, are recognizably like ourselves, in whose perceptions, responses, and fortunes we find ourselves involved, sometimes passionately, sometimes more distantly, in accordance with how these have been rendered by an author.[45] When Keats, for example, "on sitting down to read *King Lear* once again," tells us that he must "burn through" the "dispute / Betwixt damnation and impassion'd clay," we know from experience what it is to read Shakespeare's drama of human tragedy in this intensely responsive way. And when Byron, on looking into his comic poem *Don Juan*, cries elatedly to his friend Douglas Kinnaird, "Confess—confess, you dog, and be candid. . . . It may be profligate, but is it not *life*, is it not *the thing*?"[46] we recognize what it is for a represented literary world to seem no less actual and vital than the life we live. On the other hand, when Roland Barthes asserts that "what goes on in a narrative is, from the referential (real) point of view, strictly *nothing*," but "what does 'happen' is language *per se*, the adventure of language," it is grossly inapposite to the common reader's engagement with the experiences of the purposive, fallible, perplexed, and feelingful persons that a literary narrative—"stubbornly referential" as Clara Claiborne Park has said[47]—often compels.

In a recent interview Derrida remarked that, although

interested by "fictionality," "I must confess that deep down I have probably never drawn great enjoyment from fiction, from reading novels for example, beyond the pleasure taken in analyzing the play of writing, or else certain naïve movements of identification. . . . Telling or inventing stories is something that deep down (or rather on the surface!) does not interest me particularly."[48] As an autobiographical fact, fair enough; but in critical commentaries on literature, to deal with a text solely as a "play of writing," exclusive of the "story"—exclusive, that is, of the characters, actions, thoughts, and feelings, in the distinctive way these matters are signified and rendered in the particular instance—is to strip the text of its human dimension and its potent source of human interest and involvement. It is interesting to speculate what Chaucer, or Molière, or Tolstoy might have said, if confronted by the recommendation of some writers who have translated Derrida's deconstructive theory into an applied criticism, that the unillusioned way to read their literary texts is to follow the action of the warring internal forces as they contort into aporias without solutions and open out a semantic regress into abysses without bottoms.

I find unrecognizable, and also off-putting, the world projected in the latter-day critical writings of Paul de Man, in which the human subject is so entirely textualized that all the "subjectivities" of human experience are reduced—or more precisely *redacted*, by intricate interpretive maneuvers—to the possibility that they are generated by the machine-like functioning and arbitrary violences of language in itself, to the extent that death itself can be described as "a displaced name for a linguistic predicament."[49] A telling example is provided by de Man's reading of Rousseau's *Confessions*. At the end of a tortuous—and in its early stages, illuminating—analysis of the relation between feeling guilt and offering excuses for the action that has provoked the guilt, de Man concludes: "It is no longer certain that language, as excuse, exists because of a prior guilt but just as possible that since language, as a machine, performs anyway, we have to produce guilt (and all its train of psychic consequences) in order to make the excuse meaningful. Excuses generate the very guilt they exonerate, though always in excess or by default."[50] Bleakly inhuman also, although reached by a different conceptual route, is the theory world in the writings of Michel Foucault and some of his critical followers—when presented not as a speculative standpoint but as an undeluded view of the way things really are—in which people are bodies whose subjectivities are no more than functions of the subject-positions imposed by the discourse of their era; a world not only without effective human purposes but also without feelings, whether of love and sympathy or of contempt and hate, traversed only by an impersonal and unpersoned "power." From the viewpoint of ordinary human engagement, some way-out poststructural writings in the critical journals seem not only abstract but alien, as though written by extraterrestrials who have somehow learned to deploy a human vocabulary without participating in the forms of life with which the vocabulary is integral.

As described by J. Hillis Miller, "the deconstructive critic seeks to find . . . the element in the system studied which is alogical, the thread in the text in question which will unravel it all, or the loose stone which will pull down the whole building."[51] Such a statement highlights a feature shared by some deconstructive critics with exponents of other poststructural modes with whom they are often in conflict. That is, they concur in the theoretical predetermination that no author can say what he really means and that no text can mean what it seems to say—not merely in this or that instance, but universally, *überhaupt*, whether (as in Paul de Man's version of this view) because of a duplicity that is "a necessity dictated or controlled by the very nature of all critical language,"[52] or else because of subversive motives and desires that are inscribed in the unconscious of all authors and readers, or because of distortive ideological or cultural formations that saturate all discourse, or because of the irreparable incapacity of the "historical unconscious" to come to expression, or (in the writings of some eclectic theorists) because of all the above. In this last instance, the result can be a hermeneutics of suspicion so relentless that it approximates a hermeneutics of paranoia. Instead of engaging with what an author's imagination has set forth, the reader looks askance at a literary work, with the interpretive attitude: What's this text trying to put over on me?

I can bring to bear a second consideration against radical poststructural theories; namely, that the theory world, in addition to being unbelievable, is uninhabitable by the theorist himself. In the everyday conduct of life, when something turns up that engages a theorist's moral or political or personal concerns, he abandons theory talk for the ordinary human-centered talk about intentional persons, what they say and mean, and their intellectual and moral responsibility for what they have said. The divergence between a theorist's general claims and his engaged discursive practice is especially evident when his theory itself is contested by a theorist of an alternative persuasion. In such instances— an example is the published controversy between Derrida and Foucault—the reports that the subject is only a linguistic effect, or that the author is dead, turn out to have been exaggerated; for the author-subject revives, rescued from the half-life of the *sous rature*, divested of quotation marks and other disclaimers, and reinvested with such logocentric, or else bourgeois, attributes as an initiating purpose, a decidable intention to mean what he says, and very human motives and feelings. Or rather, two authors revive. One is the indignant theorist whose views have been described and challenged, and the other is the opponent theorist, whom he charges with having misread the obvious meanings of his texts, out of carelessness, or obtuseness, or (it is often implied) for less reputable reasons. Whatever the theoretical bearings of the radical questioning, in Derrida's writings, of such concepts as truth, the binary opposition true/false, and the decidability of an intention to mean something, he makes it clear that such theoretical considerations are entirely compatible with his own downright uses of the problematic concepts in the give-and-take of actual discourse. In a recent dispute with Jürgen Habermas, for example, he asserts: "That is false. I say *false* as opposed to *true*, and I defy Habermas to prove the presence in my work of that 'primacy of rhetoric' which he attributes to me."[53]

In an extensive response to a question about "the practical implications for interpretation" of his general views about language, Derrida explains his readiness, in particular discursive occasions such as his response to Habermas, to interpret decidably and to assert the truth of what someone has said or written. He relies, he says, on "a relative stability of the dominant interpretation," and on "a very solid zone of implicit 'conventions' or 'contracts'" that allows him to count on "a very strong probability of consensus concerning the intelligibility of a text." He makes the further point that within such "interpretive contexts . . . that are relatively stable, sometimes apparently almost unshakable, it should be possible to invoke rules of competence, criteria of discussion and of consensus, good faith," and the other values "associated with" the "value of truth." In explaining the assurance of his own interpretive practice in an essay attacking South African apartheid and in a later defense of that essay, Derrida points out that even though "there is no stability that is absolute, eternal, intangible, natural, etc.," yet "I consider the context of [a] discussion, like that of this one, to be very stable and very determined." Thus it

> constitutes the object of agreements sufficiently confirmed so that one might *count* [*tabler*] on ties that are stable, and hence demonstrable, linking words, concepts and things, as well as

on the difference between the true and the false. And hence one is able, in this context, to denounce errors, and even dishonesty and confusions. . . . [But] the context is only relatively stable. The ties between words, concepts, and things, truth and reference, are not *absolutely* and purely guaranteed by some metacontextuality or metadiscursivity.[54]

In these passages I take Derrida to assert, among other things, the following: In the engaged practice of language, the possibility for an assured interpretive decision is provided by the existence of a stable context, shared by writer and interpreters, of linguistic, institutional, and other conventions and agreements; this stability, however, is never entirely and unalterably fixed, nor can we guarantee the certainty and truth of any interpretation by reference to an absolute and eternal criterion beyond the regularities of our shared linguistic practice; hence one's assurance about an interpretation and its truth is never an absolute certainty, since it always remains possible (although in some instances exceedingly unlikely) that one has got it wrong. And if I interpret Derrida rightly, then—on this matter of how, in actual practice, we are able to accomplish and to justify decidable interpretations—I agree with him; and I would hazard that no current philosopher of language who takes his theoretical stand in the paradigm of language as interpersonal communication would, in any essential way, disagree with him. But if so, the question arises: What is the import for our linguistic practice of Derrida's theoretical claim that the differential constitution of language "a priori, always and already," as I quoted him, "leaves us no choice" but to say something other than what we meant to say, and to understand something other than what was said?—except, perhaps, as a salutary admonition to remember that it is always possible that we are mistaken.

J. Hillis Miller, notable among the critics who have converted

Derrida's grammatology into a method of reading literature, exemplifies the conspicuous disparity between the way a deconstructor interprets literary texts and the way he or she practices interpretation in the exigencies of everyday life. In Miller's presidential address to the Modern Language Association in 1986, he countered what he called "attacks" on deconstruction in texts written both by conservative critics on the right and by neo-Marxists and new historians on the left. Someone coming to Miller's address directly from reading his essays in literary criticism might reasonably suppose that he would respond by teasing out the loose thread in an opponent's text that will unravel, and so render both self-conflicting and undecidable, what the opponent mistakenly thinks he is decidably saying against deconstruction. Instead, however, Miller responded by the unqualified assertion that the many representatives of "the left and right are often united . . . in their misrepresentation, their shallow understanding, and their failure to have read what they denounce or their apparent inability to make out its plain sense." Miller then went on, in a disabling tactic often used in the defense of deconstruction, to attribute the real motivation of such "misreadings" not to disagreements in principle, but to "the anxiety of the accusers" who "need to point the finger of blame against theory to avoid thinking through the challenge theory poses to their own ideologies."[55]

Now, let's suppose that by the considerations I have expounded (heightened, as my exposition obviously has been, by persuasive rhetoric) I were to convince a poststructural critic that his theory not only implicates an unrecognizable world but implies a linguistic practice that is conspicuously at odds with his own usage in everyday life. It would be a mistake to assume that, in such an event, a confirmed poststructuralist would consider himself compelled to give up, or even drastically to alter, his theory. There is the exemplary instance of David Hume that I alluded to earlier. Hume finds that the skeptical theory world of his solitary speculations is utterly incongruent with the ordinary world in which he plays backgammon and converses with his friends; also, that he cannot live his skepticism, while he cannot but live in the human world. These findings, however, don't lead him to abandon his theory; instead he asserts that he lives, and also recommends to his readers, a double life. "Here then I find myself absolutely and necessarily determin'd to live, and talk, and act like other people in the common affairs of life." Yet "in all the incidents of [that] life we ought still to preserve our skepticism. If we believe, that fire warms, or water refreshes, 'tis only because it costs us too much pain to think otherwise."[56] In a comparable way Jacques Derrida—asseverating that iterability, as the necessary condition that makes language possible, thereby renders it impossible, and that deconstruction can neither escape nor replace the logocentrism it subverts, nor supersede the built-in humanism of Western thought it tries to go beyond, nor dispense with reading determinately even while affirming the essential undecidability of meaning—describes deconstruction as "a double gesture, a double science, a double writing," in which the term "double" designates "a sort of irreducible divisibility" that must "inevitably . . . continue (up to a certain point) to respect the rules of that which it deconstructs."[57] In an alternative figure Derrida, like Hume, represents the deconstructive interpreter as living a double life: there are today "two interpretations of interpretation—which are absolutely irreconcilable even if we live them simultaneously and reconcile them in an obscure economy"; and between these "I do not believe that today there is any question of *choosing*."[58] Against this view that the condition of language makes it self-deconstruct even as it constructs, so that a "rigorous" reading cannot but deconstruct even as it construes, I can, in the last resort, only reassert the alternative view from the world of language-in-use and then go on to affirm the kind of literary criticism that is positioned in this setting of human engagement.

This brings me, at the close, to put forward this answer to the question posed in my title: A humanistic literary criticism is one that deals with a work of literature as composed by a human being, for human beings, and about human beings and matters of human concern.

To guard against misunderstanding, I add three brief comments. This proposal is not meant to be in any way novel, but simply to epitomize the frame of reference shared by the critics who, historically, have mattered most, in the broad temporal and cultural range from Aristotle and Horace to Edmund Wilson and Northrop Frye. Furthermore, to identify a critical procedure as humanistic is not to warrant either its validity or its value. There is good humanistic criticism and bad humanistic criticism, to the extent, among other things, that it is perceptive, cogent, enlightening, and responsible, as against routine, pointless, obfuscative, and irresponsible. Finally, the criteria I propose are minimal, in the sense that they leave everything of substance still to be said in the unceasing, diverse, and unpredictable dialogue, without finality, of readers with literary works and of readers with each other that has constituted criticism in the civilized past, and, I am confident, will do so in the future.

NOTES

1. Claude Lévi-Strauss, *La Pensée sauvage* (Paris, 1962), p. 326. Eugenio Donato, "Of Structuralism and Literature," *Modern Language Notes* 82 (1967): 556. *Roland Barthes par Roland Barthes* (Paris, 1975), pp. 60, 82. Jacques Derrida, "Structure, Sign and Play in the Discourse of the Human Sciences," in *The Languages of Criticism and the Sciences of Many*, edited by Richard Macksey and Eugenio Donato (Baltimore and London, 1970), p. 264, and "Afterword," in *Limited Inc.*, edited by Gerald Graff (Evanston, Ill., 1988), p. 134. Michel Foucault, *The Order of Things* (London, 1970), pp. xxiii, 342–43.
2. William V. Spanos, *The End of Education: Toward Posthumanism*

(Minneapolis and London, 1993); see the "Introduction," pp. xiii–xxiv.

3. Paul de Man, "Shelley Disfigured," in *The Rhetoric of Humanism* (New York, 1984), p. 116. Another theorist of deconstruction, Hillis Miller, described "theory" as "an orientation to language as such" ("The Triumph of Theory, the Resistance to Reading, and the Question of the Material Base," *PMLA* 102 [1987]: 283).

4. Roland Barthes, "The Death of the Author (1968)," in *Image/Music/Text*, translated by Stephen Heath (New York, 1977), pp. 145–47. The hand of the "scriptor," Barthes remarks, "borne by a pure gesture of inscription . . . traces a field" which "has no other origin than language itself" (p. 46).

5. Derrida in *The Languages of Criticism*, pp. 271–72; *Positions*, translated by Alan Bass (Chicago, 1981), pp. 28–29; *Of Grammatology*, translated by Gayatri Chakravorty Spivak (Baltimore and London, 1976), p. 99. Paul de Man proposes that we "free ourselves of all false questions of intent and rightfully reduce the narrator to the status of a mere grammatical pronoun, without which the narrative could not come into being" (*Allegories of Reading* [New Haven and London, 1979], p. 18).

6. Roland Barthes, "An Introduction to the Structural Analysis of Narrative," *New Literary History* 6 (1975): 271; and "The Death of the Author," in *Image/Music/Text*, p. 146. (See also Barthes' essay "From Work to Text," in *Textual Strategies: Perspectives in Post-Structuralist Theory*, edited by Josué V. Harari [Ithaca, N.Y., 1979], pp. 73–81.) Jacques Derrida, *Positions*, p. 66; "Signature, Event, Context," in *Limited Inc.*, pp. 3, 19, 20.

7. Jonathan Culler, *Roland Barthes* (New York, 1983), pp. 81–82.

8. Barbara Johnson, *The Critical Difference* (Baltimore and London, 1980), pp. 143–44.

9. John Searle, "Reiterating the Differences: A Reply to Derrida," *Glyph* 1 (1977): 201–2.

10. Derrida, "The Supplement of Origin," in *Speech and Phenomena*, translated by David B. Allison (Evanston, Ill., 1973), pp. 93, 96. "Signature, Event, Context," in *Limited Inc.*, pp. 3, 8, 11, 20.

11. Derrida, *Of Grammatology*, pp. 158–59; see also p. 163. For his explanation that in these passages he intended to "recast the concept of

text by generalizing it almost without meaning," see his essay "But, beyond . . . ," *Critical Inquiry* 13 (1986): 167–68.

12. Derrida, "Afterword," *Limited Inc.*, p. 137; *Of Grammatology*, p. 159.

13. Barbara Johnson, *A World of Difference* (Baltimore, 1987), p. 45.

14. Derrida, "Letter to a Japanese Friend," in *Derrida and "Différance,"* edited by David Wood and Robert Bernasconi (Evanston, Ill., 1988), pp. 3–4. See also Hillis Miller: "Deconstruction is not a dismantling of the text but a demonstration that the text has already dismantled itself" ("Stevens' Rock and Criticism as Cure," *The Georgia Review* 30 [1976]: 335–36).

15. Roland Barthes, *"Texte, théorie du,"* in the *Encyclopaedia universalis* as cited by Culler, *Roland Barthes*, p. 118; "The Death of the Author," p. 143.

16. Michel Foucault, *Power/Knowledge*, edited by Colin Gordon (New York, 1980), pp. 98–119.

17. Stephen Greenblatt, "Introduction," *Representing the English Renaissance* (Berkeley, Calif., 1988), p. viii.

18. Foucault, "The Discourse on Language," in *The Archeology of Knowledge* (New York, 1972), p. 229, and *The Foucault Reader*, edited by Paul Rabinow (New York, 1984), pp. 56–57.

19. Derrida, *Of Grammatology*, p. 112; and "Aphorism Countertime," in *Acts of Literature*, edited by Derek Attridge (New York and London, 1992), pp. 416–33. Paul de Man, *Allegories of Reading*, p. 296.

20. Derrida, *Of Grammatology*, pp. 157–58. J. Hillis Miller, *Fiction and Repetition: Seven English Novels* (Cambridge, Mass., 1982), p. 53.

21. de Man, *Allegories of Reading*, pp. ix, 131. Johnson, *The Critical Difference*, p. 5.

22. Barthes, "The Death of the Author," pp. 142–48. Michel Foucault, "What Is an Author?" (1969), in *The Foucault Reader*, pp. 101–20.

23. Foucault, "What Is an Author?" pp. 107–11, 118–19.

24. Barthes, "The Death of the Author," pp. 142–43, 146–47.

25. Barthes, "The Death of the Author," pp. 142–43. Foucault, "What Is an Author?," pp. 101, 108–9, 119.

26. Foucault, "What Is an Author?" p. 108.

27. In his Epistle I.xx.1–2, Horace whimsically charges his book with an unseemly eagerness to hurry to the business district of the booksellers, in order to be exposed to sale.

28. See Frederick G. Kenyon, *Books and Readers in Ancient Greece and Rome*, 2nd ed. (Oxford, 1950), especially pp. 81–84.

29. For a discussion of the shifting emphasis, within the historical frame of critical discussions, on the world, the audience, and the work itself, see M. H. Abrams, *The Mirror and the Lamp* (New York, 1953), chapter 1, "Orientation of Critical Theories."

30. René Descartes, *Meditations on the First Philosophy*, Meditations 1 and 2.

31. David Hume, *A Treatise of Human Nature*, edited by L. A. Selby-Bigge (Oxford, 1928), pp. 264, 269–71.

32. Ludwig Wittgenstein, *Philosophical Investigations*, translated by G. E. M. Anscombe (Oxford, 1953), nos. 217, 325–26; and p. 226. *On Certainty*, edited by G. E. M. Anscombe and G. H. von Wright (New York and Evanston, Ill., 1969), pp. 162, 204, 358.

33. Wittgenstein, *On Certainty*, pp. 105, 151, 162.

34. John Keats, *The Fall of Hyperion*, canto 1, line 304.

35. For example, David Hume, when writing as a literary critic and not a philosophical skeptic, takes a stance within the humanistic frame of reference. See his essay "Of Tragedy" (1757), which discusses tragedy as "an imitation of human actions," and asserts that "the whole art of the poet is employed in rousing and supporting the compassion and indignation, the anxiety and resentment, of his audience."

36. Derrida, "Force and Signification," in *Writing and Difference*, translated by Alan Bass (Chicago, 1978), pp. 3–30.

37. Derrida, "White Mythology: Metaphor in the Text of Philosophy," *New Literary History* 6 (1974): 5–74.

38. For example, "White Mythology," p. 13: "The task is . . . to dismantle the metaphysical and rhetorical structures which are at work . . . not in order to reject or discard them, but to reconstitute them in another way." And "Afterword," *Limited Inc.*, p. 146: "The value of truth (and of all those values associated with it) is never contested or destroyed in my writings, but only reinscribed in more powerful, larger, more stratified contexts."

39. Johnson, *A World of Difference*, pp. xvii–xviii.

40. Richard Rorty, "Is Derrida a Transcendental Philosopher?" *Yale Journal of Criticism* 2 (1989): 207, 215. See also Rorty, "Philosophy as a Kind of Writing: An Essay on Derrida," in *Consequences of Pragmatism* (Minneapolis, 1982).

41. Derrida, *Limited Inc.*, pp. 61–62; "Afterword," p. 129.

42. Wittgenstein, *On Certainty*, p. 92. On some notable philosophical conversion experiences to a radically different initiating position, see M. H. Abrams, "Coleridge and the Romantic Vision of the World," *The Correspondent Breeze* (New York and London, 1984), pp. 199–206.

43. Goethe, *Dichtung und Wahrheit*, Part III, Book xi.

44. James Boswell, *The Life of Samuel Johnson*, entry for 1763.

45. Experimental and postmodernist types of "metafiction" that undertake to dispense with recognizable characters, setting, and sequential narrative are second-order literary productions, in that they achieve their specific effects by presupposing, in order to frustrate, readers' expectations based on traditional modes of fiction.

46. Byron, letter to Douglas Kinnaird, October 26, 1819.

47. Barthes, "An Introduction to the Structural Analysis of Narrative," *New Literary History* 6 (1975): 271. Clara Claiborne Park, *Rejoining the Common Reader* (Evanston, Ill., 1991), p. 227.

48. Derrida, "This Strange Institution Called Literature" (1989), in *Acts of Literature*, edited by Derek Attridge (New York and London, 1992), pp. 39–40. Later in the interview Derrida said, "One of the main reasons for my interest in literature" is that it "teaches us more, and even the 'essential,' about writing in general" (pp. 71–72).

49. de Man, "Autobiography as Defacement," in *The Rhetoric of Romanticism*, p. 81.

50. de Man, *Allegories of Reading*, p. 199. In a related discussion of the representation of guilt by Proust, de Man asserts that "no one can decide whether Proust invented metaphors because he felt guilty or whether he had to declare himself guilty in order to find a use for metaphor"; he adds, "The second hypothesis is in fact less unlikely than the first."

51. J. H. Miller, "Stevens' Rock and Criticism as Cure, II," *Georgia Review* 30 (1976): 341.

52. de Man, *Blindness and Insight*, p. 111. Also de Man's *Allegories of Reading*, p. 277: An author, "just as any other reader . . . is bound to misread his text. . . . Language itself dissociates the cognition from the act."

53. Derrida, "Afterword," *Limited Inc.*, p. 157. Derrida is responding to Habermas' attack in *The Philosophical Discourse of Modernity* (1987).

54. Derrida, "Afterword," *Limited Inc.*, pp. 143–44, 146, 151.

55. J. H. Miller, "The Triumph of Theory," *PMLA* 102 (1987): 284.

56. Hume, *A Treatise of Human Nature*, pp. 269–70.

57. Derrida, *Limited Inc.*, pp. 21, 152.

58. Derrida, "Structure, Sign, and Play," in *The Languages of Criticism*, pp. 264–65.

The Language and
Methods of Humanism

I FIND ENLIGHTENING AND useful Frederick Olafson's sketch of the conceptual scheme—the frame of often implicit assumptions—that has been a distinctive feature within the various disciplines traditionally grouped as "the humanities." This scheme establishes coordinates that enable us, in a preliminary way, to map out what is humanistic, what is nonhumanistic, and what is antihumanistic; it also enables us to detect recent tendencies within the humanities themselves that threaten to subvert, or else to abandon silently, the very premises on which the Western humanist, through the centuries, has undertaken to understand

From *The Philosophy of the Curriculum: The Need for General Education*, edited by Sidney Hook, Paul Kurtz, and Miro Todorovich (Buffalo, N.Y., 1975). This was a paper delivered at a conference on "The Philosophy of the Curriculum" held at Rockefeller University in 1973. References are to two papers published in the same volume: Frederick A. Olafson, "Humanism and the Humanities," and Gertrude Himmelfarb, "Observations on Humanism and History."

and assess man, his actions, his history, and his intellectual and imaginative productions.

Olafson finds that the traditional humanistic concern is with the world of the distinctive person, for whom nonhuman nature is the theater for his activities, and who confronts in the world other persons similarly endowed and engaged. These persons are thinking and feeling agents who manifest intentions and purposes and have some measure of control over, and thus responsibility for, their own destinies. If there is purpose, there is also a choice between alternative actions, and the choice and its consequences can be judged by criteria of better or worse, right or wrong, good or evil. Human life and history are viewed as a narrative sequence, or drama, in which there are conflicts within a person, and between persons, and between a person and the conditions of his milieu. This drama, as it evolves, displays love and hate, mutual achievements and mutual destruction, individual successes and failures, comedy and tragedy, the sublime and the ridiculous. In his intellectual and imaginative products, man expresses his human concern—his "form of life," his informing vision, his assumptions and structure of values—and the humanist scholar who undertakes to understand and place and assess these products views them, ultimately, through his own perspective of concern.

What I want to do is bring these traditional humanistic concepts to bear on two topics that have emerged at this conference. The first topic is the risk of skepticism and relativism to the modern humanistic enterprises; the second is the question of whether effective teaching in a liberal education is primarily a teaching of "arts" and methods in the humanistic disciplines, or whether it is primarily a teaching by example, by instancing in the person of the individual humanist a stance and procedure that is representatively humanistic.

I

The humanist typically addresses himself to texts that are not written in the highly refined and specialized languages of the logician or the scientist, but in the ordinary language that has been developed over many centuries to express and to deal with the complexities, the ambiguities, the nuances, and the contradictions of the human predicament—the predicament of purposive, fallible, perplexed, and feeling persons, who, for better or worse, act and interact and manifest what Keats called "the fierce dispute / Between damnation and impassioned clay." Also, the traditional language of humanistic critics and scholars, despite some technical elements specific to a particular discipline, remains the ordinary language of the persons and documents with which they deal—and it has to do so if humanists are to carry out their traditional functions.

From this fact follows a conclusion that some of us find hard to accept; namely, that in many of the central and most distinctive judgments of the humanistic scholar and critic we can never achieve certainty. In fact, one way to identify the humanities is to say that they are those disciplines whose concern is with the areas of human action and production where valid knowledge is the aim, where a rational procedure is essential, but where certainty is impossible.

I agree with Gertrude Himmelfarb's concern about the dangers to the humanities of threats from within—the threats of radical skepticism and relativism, and of giving up the old search for truth. I recognize—with equal dismay—the same tendencies in literary studies that she finds in historical studies: a surrender to irrationality, a stress on multiple "interps" instead of meaning, the drift to a profound skepticism, even to nihilism, with respect to values. It would be a bad mistake, however, to combat such tendencies by the counterclaim that humanistic studies, in all their central enterprises, can yield certainty and a single and ultimate truth. Some parts—some basic parts—of these studies are indeed factual, and therefore subject to the criteria that govern the sciences: the criteria of valid empirical reasoning and the established ways to support or falsify hypotheses. But when you get down to matters of explanation, interpretation, and evaluation—whether of *Hamlet* or of Aristotle's *Poetics* or of the French Revolution or of the nature of justice—then you are out of the realm where certainty is possible and where universal, or even very widespread, agreement is to be found.

Even when I, as a literary critic, feel quite certain that I am asserting the truth about a complex work, I have long since given up being surprised to find that other commentators, who are indubitably expert, sensitive, and rational critics, sharply disagree. If we should be so misguided as to claim to our students that in this realm our conclusions are certain and at least approximate the single and universal truth of the matter, then we shall be quickly found out and discredited, with the risk of discrediting as well the whole humanistic enterprise in which we are engaged.

But I do not believe that the denial of certainty entails radical skepticism and relativism. To say that the humanist operates in a realm where, in large part, certainty and the single truth is impossible is not to say that it is a realm where uncertainty reigns, where no truths are achievable and therefore anything goes. What produces confusion in the use of the terms "certainty" and "truth" is that, in professional discourse about rational procedures, they are closely tied to highly specialized verbal and symbolic models. In the distant past, when divine authority yielded the ultimate certainty, there was also a symbolic enterprise—formal logic— that was the model of the certainty that could be achieved by human endeavor. When what we think of as modern science developed, apologists had a difficult time justifying the validity of their new systematic procedures, and they tried to mitigate the differences from the deductive logical model by bridge-concepts such as the law of sufficient reason. But after the exact sciences had triumphantly established their own validity and authority, the codified rules of scientific language and scientific reasoning achieved a status equivalent to that of logic in guaranteeing certainty, in the sense that all qualified practitioners would consent to its conclusions.

The criterion of certainty, as applied to the humanities, is usually tied to one or both of these alien and highly specialized models for achieving formal certainty or practical certainty, deductive truths or empirical truths. The language of the traditional humanist, however, is very different from the specially developed, sharply defined, and strictly rule-bound ideal languages of logic or the natural sciences. For the humanist's language, although responsible to the formal rules of logic and in its own fashion empirical, must perform its central functions beyond the point where these simplified calculi of logic and the exact sciences come to a stop. To achieve its traditional aims, the language of the humanist is necessarily flexible, loose, uncodified, nuanced, and lacking sharp definitional boundaries. Ultimately, it is also what Olafson calls the language of concern—that is, it engages with its subject matter in an area in which it is subject only to such soft-focus criteria as good sense, tact, insight, aesthetic sensibility, and a sound sense of moral values. Such discourse is rarely capable of rigid codification, and therefore rarely capable of achieving strictly conclusive arguments; but it can and should be responsible and rational—with the kind of rationality that alone is adapted to fulfill its own humane purposes and to achieve sound knowledge in its elected area of understanding. And if (when judged by the alien criteria of simplified calculi) it is not certain, neither is it, strictly speaking, uncertain. The reasoning and conclusions of humanistic discourse are subject to criteria, but these are criteria appropriate to its own intellectual enterprise, such as coherent or incoherent, inclusive or omissive, sensible or outré, disinterested or partisan, central or overly ingenious, clear or obfuscative, sound or unsound.

"The kind of certainty," Wittgenstein has said, "is the kind of language-game."[1] Now we can, if we choose, apply the word "certain" to a humanistic conclusion that satisfies the positive criteria I have listed. But if we are to avoid confusion and error, we must keep in mind that this is often a very different kind of certainty from the formal certainty of logic or the practical certainty of an exact science. An even more serious error is to try to make the humanities capable of the scientific kind of certainty by "objectifying" (to use Olafson's term) humanistic inquiry; that is, by substituting for its ordinary, loose, and flexible language of interpretation, evaluation, and concern the specialized and codified language of science and, above all, by translating the language of purpose and responsibility into a calculus of causality. Either this translation is no more than a merely lexical substitution, which results in scientism—a simulacrum of scientific procedure and conclusions—or else it is inherently incapable of accomplishing the central humanistic functions. For the language of science has achieved its precision, the codified rigor of its reasoning, and its kind of certainty by systematically eliminating from consideration all those aspects of human experience and judgment that, to the humanist and to all of us with our human interests and concerns, matter most. And when the humanist genuinely commits himself to a language modeled on that of the sciences, he finds that the specifically human aspects of his subject matter, such as individual personality, purpose, passion, drama, and value, ineluctably elude his linguistic grasp.

What I have said about humanistic language and rationality

does not entail a radical skepticism or relativism, but it does, I think, entail a very different thing: an essential pluralism in the humanistic pursuits. All nondogmatic humanists recognize in experience (and in practice, if not in theory, they make constant allowance for these things) profound differences in the elected cognitive perspectives, favored frames of reference, distinctive kinds of reasoning, and individual forms of sensibility in their fellow humanists. These differences permit individual inquirers, by diversely coherent and rational procedures, to produce sound but divergent conclusions about the matter in hand, whether it is *Hamlet* or the *Poetics* or the French Revolution or the nature of justice. And what each perspective does—if its application through the medium of an individual sensibility is rational—is to bring out different aspects of a subject, to locate it in a different context of relevant considerations, and to force us to see it in a way we have not seen it before.

I am as little disposed as Himmelfarb to surrender the term "truth" and to yield it up for the exclusive use of the logician and the scientist. But it is important to keep in mind that, as the kind of certainty is the kind of language game, so the kind of truth is the kind of language game too. And the truth that each of us, as individuals engaged in a common humanistic enterprise, ought to claim is not the final truth, the whole truth, and nothing but the truth; for that is to convert our disciplines into dogmas. The superposition of multiple, coherent, and rationally exploited perspectives yields a vision in depth; and this multidimensional knowledge constitutes what is the distinctive humanistic truth about a subject. If this claim implies that the humanistic search for truth is always in process and is never finished, I find nothing dismaying in such a conclusion. It is, in fact, precisely this feature that gives to our group of disciplines their importance and indispensability in the energetic intellectual life of a vital culture.

II

And now a few words about my second topic: the role of method as against personal example in teaching the humanities. I spend much of my own time in teaching method—that is, the forms of sound reasoning in a humanistic discipline, the kinds of questions that are relevant, and the nature and weight of the evidence for and against answers to these questions. This kind of teaching is essential in the academy and, I agree with Olafson, has been injuriously neglected in recent years. But here too it is important to remember that rational procedure in many humanistic areas can be identified and loosely described, but not codified; that it is thus (in the traditional distinction) an art rather than a science; and that to attempt to rigidly define and regulate what is by its nature and aim necessarily a flexible and elusive way of proceeding is to transform a humanistic process of reasoning into a calculus that systematically leaves out of account everything that really matters.

Because normative procedures in the humanities are variable and much easier to recognize than to categorize precisely, teaching by force of example is much more important than it is in logic or the sciences. Judging by my own experience as a student rather than as a teacher, I find that what has counted most has been a model of the humanist as a normative personage, who instantiates a humanity that becomes representative of what the humanities are. This model, ideally, is a composite of the stance and procedure of one's own teachers and of the great humanists of the past, who have projected their individual ethos in almost every page of the documents they have bequeathed to us. These humanists have managed to deal extraordinarily well with areas of experience in which rationality is essential but certainty is impossible, meeting concern with concern, yet maintaining an equilibrium between dogmatism and skepticism.

The tide most threatening to the traditional stance of the humanist in our own time, as Olafson has pointed out, is a reaction against skepticism by a kind of dogmatism that speaks in the vatic voice of the prophet and the visionary. The truth is that when you go to the liberal humanists, hot for certainties, you get what seem to be very dusty answers. As a result, some of our students turn increasingly to such prophets of the past as Nietzsche, or much worse, to some of the small and seedy prophets of our own day. The world of the prophet is a hot, intense world of total assurance that you have the humanistic truth, that you know what we must do to be saved—and as such, it has great contemporary appeal. In comparison with the hot world of prophecy, the world of the liberal humanist is a cool world. What we need to get our students to recognize is that the stance of the liberal humanist is a very difficult one, which takes poise and courage to maintain. It takes a secure balance and a firm will to conduct, rationally, a discipline in which many of the premises, procedures, and conclusions are essentially contestable, without surrendering either to an all-dissolving skepticism or to the inviting dogmatism of the visionary and the fanatic. Our aim, by example as well as precept, must be to show the dignity, as well as the comfort, of maintaining the humanistic poise, of searching for answers to our inescapable human problems, answers that are neither ultimate nor absolutely certain, but are the best and most rational ones we are capable of formulating.

The normative personages of the humanistic tradition, from Socrates to Solzhenitsyn, offer instances of ways to cope with the human predicament, while steering between the rocks of nihilism and the whirlpool of fanaticism. I have the hunch—I certainly have the hope—that the instinct for survival in civilized humanity is great enough to ensure the persistence of the humanistic stance which these models, each in a diverse and distinctive way, represent to us.

III

I was certain that, in the brevity and omissiveness with which I had to present my views, I would evoke counterclaims, and also that I would agree with a number of these counterclaims. Thus, I consent to the assertion that, in the humanistic disciplines, we are justified in rejecting some interpretations and arguments and conclusions out of hand. A large fraction of humanistic problems are factual, or close to factual (though these are often preparatory to the enterprise of interpretation and explanation), and here we often find ourselves capable of denying the factual claims or producing counterfacts or falsifying the hypotheses. And though the modes of humanistic rationality are diverse, we are able to recognize and reject patent irrationality, as well as overt dogma. Certainly, also, within the domain of interpretation itself we are often readily able to identify an impossible, inept, radically inadequate, or outrageously implausible interpretation. In fact, our jobs as teachers confront us again and again with such patent errors by students (not to speak of fellow critics and scholars); it is incumbent upon us to reject them and to identify the criteria by which we judge them unacceptable.

My emphasis in these remarks, however, has been on that area of interpretation that involves central principles of organization, of theme, structure, characterization, and authorial intentions (to use literature as an example). And here we find contestable conclusions, in the sense that expert, knowledgeable, sensitive, and reasonable critics come out with very different results. Take Shakespeare, for example. In our own century the interpretations of Shakespeare's plays—and the kinds of evaluation dependent on particular interpretations—have multiplied remarkably. We have eliminated very few of the alternative interpretations of earlier centuries, while adding many others. And some of the newer interpretations yield valuable insights, bringing into our ken aspects that enrich our ability to experience Shakespeare's plays in ways outside the range of even such great critics of the past as Johnson or Coleridge. Each validly innovative critic who exploits, rationally and responsibly, his distinctive perspective and frame of reference (whether Marxist, Freudian, New Critical, structuralist, or whatnot) adds depth to our perception of one or another of Shakespeare's plays; and I would not hesitate to say that each adds to our knowledge of the truth about that play.

This also bears on another question that has been raised. Given what I have said about the absence of criteria of certainty in some central humanistic enterprises—hence our frequent inability to resolve with finality differences in critical judgments and conclusions—how are we to distinguish between greater and lesser works of art? And on the pedagogical level, how are we to decide what works to teach our students?

I think it is only when we are theorizing about the humanities rather than practicing a humane discipline—only when we are writing metacriticism rather than criticism—that we are dismayed about the lack of anything approximating logical or scientific certainty in our elected province. What it comes to is this: To demand certainty in the humanities is in fact to ask for a set of codified rules and criteria such that when, say, a work of literature is presented to any expert critical intelligence, it will process the work and come out with a precise meaning and a fixed grade of value that will coincide with the meaning and evaluation arrived at by any other critical intelligence. When a humanist really faces up to these consequences of his demand for certainty, he finds such a mechanical process to be disquieting and repulsive—and with good reason, because in fact it is approximated only under an authoritarian cultural regime in which the codified rules and universal criteria are not discovered in the language and practice of individual critics but are established by edict. In our free

humanistic activities, we all take for granted the human predicament that the humanities both deal with and express, and we
manage as a matter of course, and quite well, to cope with a
situation in which tenable perspectives are diverse, individual
sensibilities and proclivities are distinctive, many judgments are
contestable, and few basic disagreements are in any final way
resolvable. The nature of that human predicament, in fact, is what
makes the free humanistic enterprise an indispensable, difficult,
and deeply and endlessly interesting pursuit.

As a matter of everyday practice, however, we in fact possess various ways for checking our individual judgments and for
establishing the difference between the better and the worse, the
greater and the lesser, by criteria that transcend our personal pre-
dilections and judgments. Chief among these is a revised form
of what used to be called the *consensus gentium*, which was considered the ultimate criterion of humanistic truth, goodness, and
beauty. In the revised form, we can state the principle in this way:
Agreement among diverse humanists as to the importance and
value of a work at any one time, and still more, the survival value
of a work—general agreement as to its importance and value over
an extended period of time—serves as a sound way to distinguish
the better from the worse and to identify which work is a classic.
The consensus that emerges when an imaginative work is viewed
from a diversity of critical perspectives and through a diversity
of sensibilities—and especially a consensus that emerges despite
radical cultural changes over many centuries—is a reliable index
to the fact that the work is central in its human concerns, broad
in its imaginative appeal, and rich in its inherent aesthetic and
other values.

As humane critics and teachers, we in fact employ such criteria as a matter of course. Thereby, we are certain that *Hamlet*
and *Twelfth Night* are greater and more worthy of attention than
The Spanish Tragedy or *Gammer Gurton's Needle*; as teachers, we

may for good reasons decide to teach the second two plays, but we do not make the mistake of letting them displace the plays of Shakespeare. But of course, expert critical consensus and survival value are no more than a prima facie index to a classic work. What matters to us as individuals is what has been called our "participation" in the work—our full intellectual, imaginative, and emotional engagement—as well as our response with concern to the author's concern, and our consent to the consent of the ages because we feel the greatness of the work up on our own pulses.

NOTES

1. Ludwig Wittgenstein, *Philosophical Investigations*, translated by G. E. M. Anscombe (Oxford, 1953), p. 224e.

How to Prove an Interpretation

—

C LAIMS ABOUT THE meaning of a poem which, a few decades ago, would have been regarded as brittle paradoxes have become serious commonplaces in critical theories. These theories are diverse in their principles and procedures, but all issue in the claim that it is necessarily the case that a poem cannot have a determinate meaning, and that no reading of a poem can be a correct reading.

I remind you of the prevalence of this view by some quotations. Harold Bloom: "Every act of reading . . . makes of interpretation a necessary misprision . . . or misreading." "There are no right

---

This was a lecture delivered at several universities, at various stages of its evolution, between 1976 and 1981. For related considerations of the nature of certainty and of the openness to disagreement in literary criticism and other humanistic enterprises, see the essays "What's the Use of Theorizing about the Arts?" (especially pp. 67–72), and "A Note on Wittgenstein and Literary Criticism" (especially pp. 84–87), in M. H. Abrams, *Doing Things with Texts: Essays in Criticism and Critical Theory* (New York, 1989).

readings." Stanley Fish: "Any procedure that attempts to determine which of a number of readings is correct will necessarily fail." Jacques Derrida: "In any text, the inescapable absence of a transcendental signified extends the . . . play of signification to infinity." Paul de Man: "We no longer take for granted that a literary text can be reduced to a finite meaning or set of meanings, but see the act of reading as an endless process in which truth and falsehood are inextricably intertwined." And J. Hillis Miller denies that "any work has a fixed, identifiable meaning. . . . Any reading can be shown to be a misreading on evidence drawn from the text itself."

It will surprise no one to hear that my position on this matter is the traditional one. I retain, that is, a stubborn predilection for finding out what a poem determinately means. I hold the view that, although the language of a poem may permit a considerable degree of interpretive freedom, we are usually able to achieve an interpretation that approximates the central or core meanings that the sentences of a poem were formed to convey. I believe also that we can adduce valid reasons which support such an interpretation against a proposed alternative. My critical interest, then, is in a correct reading rather than a misreading, or with a misreading as something to be detected and then discarded.

To support these claims, I shall examine a poem in order to isolate essential features of its meaning that have been disputed by competent readers, and then to identify the procedures for resolving the dispute which are available to traditional criticism. I choose this poem for several reasons: it is only eight lines long; it was introduced in a graduate seminar on philosophy and literature that the distinguished philosopher Max Black and I taught jointly at Cornell in 1972; and it has been subjected to diverse interpretations by a number of literary critics. The poem is a familiar one by William Wordsworth:

A slumber did my spirit seal;
I had no human fears:
She seemed a thing that could not feel
The touch of earthly years.

No motion has she now, no force;
She neither hears nor sees;
Rolled round in earth's diurnal course,
With rocks, and stones, and trees.

E. D. Hirsch, in his influential book *Validity in Interpretation* (1967), raised the issue of interpretive disagreement by reprinting excerpts from two commentaries on the second stanza of Wordsworth's poem. The first, by Cleanth Brooks, asserts that the "poet attempts to suggest something of the lover's agonized shock at the loved one's present lack of motion—of his response to her utter and horrible inertness." The second commentary, by F. W. Bateson, instead finds a "pantheistic magnificence" in the last two lines, for the dead Lucy "has become involved in the sublime processes of nature." This is a clear case of critical disagreement about an important feature of the poem, and it has often been discussed since Hirsch pointed it out. But notice that the divergence of these interpretations overlies an essential agreement. Brooks and Bateson disagree about the emotive state of mind, the attitudes and feelings, that the lyric speaker implies by his description of the situation in the second stanza. Both, however, agree that the speaker's emotive state of mind is in response to the same state of affairs: a girl who was alive in stanza 1 is dead in stanza 2.

That was also the way that just about all the critics who commented on "A Slumber" read the poem until 1965, when Hugh Sykes Davies published an essay, "Another New Poem by Wordsworth." This new poem is the old text of "A Slumber," interpreted in a radically new way. The subject of the poem, Davies proposes, is not a girl at all; instead, the subject is the poet's own spirit, identified in line 1—"A slumber did my *spirit* seal"—and the two stanzas describe a "trance-like state" of the poet's spirit—a state in which, at the close of the poem, the poet feels himself to be, in spirit, joined with the earth, and "identified with its diurnal motion."[1]

My initial response was that Davies proposes a blatant misreading of Wordsworth's poem. But as I went on, I found that Davies goes on to present detailed reasons that tell against what, following Davies, I shall call "the standard reading" of the poem (that it is about a girl who dies), and other reasons that tell in favor of his "new reading" of the poem (that it is about a trancelike state of the poet's own spirit). Davies argues modestly, and very well. Many of his reasons strike me as sound reasons, and force me to entertain seriously an interpretation I had rejected out of hand.

Let me say at once that Davies' reasons strike me as sound reasons because, as traditional readers, he and I share a frame of reference—a tacit set of principles and procedures—that we automatically put into play in making sense of the text of "A Slumber." We bring to the text, for example, the presumption that the two sentences constituting the poem are the written version of a *parole*, a poetic speech-act, composed by a particular author during a specific span of time. In this instance we have solid grounds for identifying the author as William Wordsworth, and the span of time at which the composition was undertaken and completed as 1798–99. We bring to our reading also the presumption that Wordsworth undertook to compose a text that would be determinately interpretable by qualified readers of English poetry. He did so by deploying his expertise in the practice of the English language—an ongoing practice which he had inherited, and had learned to employ from early infancy—as well as his expertise in the linguistic conventions specific to lyric poems. We also presuppose that we, as qualified readers, will be able to understand

Wordsworth's text, by deploying our expertise in the practice of interpreting the English language—a continuing practice that we, like Wordsworth, have inherited, and that we share with him; except for slight changes, over the course of two intervening centuries, which are identifiable, and so can be taken into account.

It is only because Davies and I share this frame of linguistic reference that our arguments for or against a disputed feature of the meaning of Wordsworth's poem can engage with each other on the same plane of discourse. Our tacit participation in a common interpretive practice enables each of us to give reasons for an interpretation of "A Slumber" that the other will account as sound and relevant reasons; even though neither of us may, at the end, find his opponent's reasons adequate to force him to change his interpretive decision.

To turn back to the issue between us: Davies claims that Wordsworth's poem is about a trancelike condition of the poet's spirit. I claim that it is about a girl who unexpectedly dies. The reasons that Davies gives for his interpretation, and the counterreasons I give for mine, I believe, pretty much exhaust the inventory of the kinds of evidence available in the attempt to resolve a radically disputed interpretation of a poem.

I

In this dispute all turns, as Davies rightly says, "on the antecedent of the pronoun 'she' in the third line." Who, or what, is "she"? In the standard reading, "she" refers to a girl; in Davies' reading, "she" refers back to the noun in line 1—the word "spirit."

The reference of "she" depends on the grammar of the English language. In my school days, teachers of English composition cited what they called a "rule" of grammar, not to use a pronoun, embedded in an utterance, except to refer to the nearest antecedent noun that agrees in number with the pronoun; and according to this rule, "she" can only refer to the noun "spirit." But such prescriptive grammatical rules are merely rules of thumb, useful as a shortcut to guiding novices to write clearly and avoid ambiguity. The validity of such rules is based on the trained intuitions—the linguistic tact—of competent users of a language; that is, on their sense of what is grammatically normal, and also what is grammatically possible. This linguistic tact is the product of our mastery, over time, of the regularities of usage in the practice of the language we have inherited.

In the seminar I have mentioned, the graduate students were asked to specify the reference of "she" in an unidentified text of "A Slumber." Of the seventeen respondents, eleven identified the referent as a girl or young woman, while six identified it as the antecedent word "spirit." That so large a minority chose the latter alternative, I admit, surprised me. I now think that Max Black and I made a mistake in specifically asking the question; the results were probably biased, because to ask canny students these days "What is the reference of 'she'?" alerts them to seek other possibilities than the one that seems obvious—it is to force a card. However that may be, I must grant that Davies has scored a sound point: if we take "A Slumber" in isolation, a possible initial expectation is that "she" refers to "spirit"; its reference to a girl not hitherto mentioned, while permitted by our grammatical tact—especially in the conventionally abrupt onset of a short lyric poem—is a slight surprise.

But to read "she" as referring to "spirit" runs counter to another intuition in our practice of the language. In English, when a noun such as "spirit" signifies something that is not clearly masculine or feminine, our expectation is that a pronoun referring to it will be not the feminine "she," but the neuter "it." If Wordsworth, then, intended to refer to "spirit," why didn't he put the reference beyond question by writing, "*It* seemed a thing . . ."?

To meet this objection, Davies appeals from what we intuit as a regularity in the general practice of a language, to an idiolect—the special practice of a particular speaker. He demonstrates that in his other poems Wordsworth, when referring to "spirit" in the sense of a human faculty, sometimes used a neuter, but at other times a feminine pronoun. While we find in some of Wordsworth's poems clear instances of the neuter pronoun (for example, "and now her Spirit longed / For *its* last flight to heaven's security"), we find in other poems clear instances of the feminine pronoun (for example, "and there his spirit shaped / *Her* prospects . . .").

Where does the twofold appeal to our linguistic tact—our trained intuition of the norms, or impulsions, of English grammar—leave us? Since each tends in a different direction, I would say that it leaves us balanced between the standard and new reading of "A Slumber." We need to seek further evidence before deciding between them.

II

Davies turns next to evidence for an author's intention. The question here becomes: Did Wordsworth intend the pronoun "she" in the third line to refer to the lyric speaker's spirit, or to a girl?

It is clear from what Hugh Sykes Davies says that he shares my view—it is the traditional view—that a successful utterance is the verbal realization of the speaker's intention to mean something, and that for a hearer or reader to grasp that intention is to understand the utterance correctly. But so long as we limit ourselves to the printed text of "A Slumber," an appeal to Wordsworth's intention will get us nowhere in deciding between our disputed interpretations. Wordsworth's intended meaning is available to us only insofar as it is successfully realized in the text. To appeal, therefore, to Wordsworth's intention in the text of "A Slumber" in order to resolve an equivocality in that text is to reason in a circle, for it appeals to an intention whose equivocality in the problem we seek to resolve.

Let us, then, look for evidence of Wordsworth's intention outside the text of "A Slumber." By "intention" I don't mean a distinctive conscious state which preceded the poet's writing of the opening lines of "A Slumber," for the poet's intended meaning gets realized only in the process of verbalizing the sentences that constitute the poem. By direct, external evidence of Wordsworth's intended meaning I signify simply what Wordsworth would have said, after composing the poem, in answer to a question about the intended reference of the pronoun "she."

Suppose we were to find a letter written in 1799 by Wordsworth's friend and fellow poet, S. T. Coleridge, in which he reports asking Wordsworth, "William, in the third line of 'A Slumber,' what did you intend the pronoun 'she' to refer to?" and that Wordsworth had answered, "I meant a girl, of course." Since that response comports with the phrasing of the text of "A Slumber," that would settle the matter. If on the other hand Wordsworth had said, "I meant by 'she' my own spirit," that would also settle the matter. In response to this latter possibility, however, Coleridge might well have said: "Well, yes; but you were careless in your phrasing, because I, like most others who read your poem, take 'she' to refer to a girl." (We know that is the way Coleridge interpreted the pronoun, because in a letter written in 1799, after receiving a manuscript copy of "A Slumber," he described it as "a most sublime epitaph.")

Hugh Sykes Davies in his essay asserts, as I have, that if we had a direct and credible statement from Wordsworth that he intended "she" to refer to a girl, "that would be an end of the matter"; but he points out that we have no such direct statement from Wordsworth. We do, however, possess indirect evidence, outside

the text of "A Slumber," of Wordsworth's authorial intention, and
that is the seeming fact that Wordsworth wrote "A Slumber" as
one in a group of five poems, in which the other four poems refer
indubitably to the death—actual or anticipated—of a girl, who in
each of these poems is named "Lucy." If so, this would constitute
evidence that Wordsworth intended "A Slumber" to be one of five
lyric meditations on the unexpected death of a girl.

Davies argues strenuously against the grounds of the assumption that Wordsworth intended "A Slumber" to be a Lucy poem.
We can see why he needs to do so. In Wordsworth's first publication of "A Slumber" in *Lyrical Ballads* of 1800, and in the subsequent editions of 1802 and 1805, "A Slumber" is preceded by two
poems explicitly about the death of Lucy, of which the second is
"She Dwelt among th' Untrodden Ways." The readers of these
volumes thus found the following sequence from the last stanza
of "She Dwelt" to the first stanza of "A Slumber." There is no title
to break this sequence; only a printer's ruled line:

> She lived unknown, and few could know
>   When Lucy ceased to be;
> But she is in her grave, and, oh,
>   The difference to me!
>
> ———————————
>
> A slumber did my spirit seal;
>   I had no human fears:
> She seemed a thing that could not feel
>   The touch of earthly years.

If we read this as Wordsworth's deliberately planned sequence,
there seems little room for doubt that the "she" in "A Slumber"
was intended to be synonymous in reference with the "she" in the
preceding stanza, and that this she "is in her grave."

Davies' arguments against identifying "A Slumber" as a poem

about Lucy is threefold: (1) It alone in the group of five doesn't include the name of "Lucy," nor even mention a girl. (2) Wordsworth never printed more than three of the so-called Lucy poems together; the standard conjunction of all five is the work of nineteenth-century editors and anthologists of Wordsworth's poetry. (3) In his edition of his *Poems* in 1815, fifteen years after the initial publication of "A Slumber," Wordsworth took the poem out of its earlier conjunction with two Lucy poems, and instead placed it after a different Lucy poem, "Three Years She Grew," in a section of his volume that he classified as "Poems of the Imagination." From these indubitable facts, Davies proposes the conclusion that Wordsworth had never intended "A Slumber" to be a poem about Lucy, nor an elegy. He printed it next to one or more of the Lucy poems only because of the incidental circumstance that all these poems had been written in 1799, while Wordsworth was living in Germany.

These arguments seem a case of special pleading. This aspect comes clear if we restate the same facts with a contrary emphasis: Wordsworth *always* published "A Slumber" in combination with at least one poem explicitly about the fact or premonition of Lucy dying, and he always placed it immediately *after* the Lucy poem or poems. Thus, even in the altered position in the volume of 1815, we get the following sequence of the closing stanza of "Three Years She Grew" and the opening stanza of "A Slumber":

Thus Nature spake—The work was done—
How soon my Lucy's race was run!
She died, and left to me
This heath, this calm, and quiet scene;
The memory of what has been,
And never more will be.

A slumber did my spirit seal. . . .

It is to a high degree unlikely that Wordsworth, with his care about the order in which to print his poems, would in every instance place a poem, intended to be about a trancelike state of his spirit, in a position where the grammatical reach of "she" is so patently back to "Lucy" in the preceding stanza.

Where do we stand now? I think it fair to say that the indirect evidence of Wordsworth's intention, like the evidence of grammatical norms in the first stanza, still leaves the possibility open—but much less open—that the poem is about the poet's spirit. Where do we turn for further evidence?

III

Davies' next move is to adduce a number of passages from Wordsworth's other poems which represent a trancelike state of the poet's spirit, with the claim that they closely parallel "A Slumber," in that they describe that state in terms that are identical, or closely related to, central terms in "A Slumber."

I agree that if Davies' parallel passages are close, and close in the most telling ways to "A Slumber," they strengthen the case for his reading of the poem, on the ground that, if Wordsworth habitually uses certain terms to describe trance states, the presence of those terms in "A Slumber" enhance the likelihood that this poem is also about a trance state. The trouble, however, is that each of Davies' parallel passages does not coincide with, but instead lies askew to, the meaning he ascribes to "A Slumber," in a way that casts substantial doubt on its pertinence for establishing the meaning of Wordsworth's poem.

I present as examples three of Davies' passages which are the strongest of his proposed parallels. The first two are from Wordsworth's *The Prelude* of 1805, in the sequence that Davies gives them:

> Wonder not
> If such my transports were; for in all things
> I saw one life, and felt that it was joy.
> One song they sang, and it was audible,
> Most audible then when the fleshly ear,
> O'ercome by grosser prelude of that strain,
> Forgot its functions, and slept undisturb'd.
>
> * * *
>
> Oft in those moments such a holy calm
> Did overspread my soul, that I forgot
> That I had bodily eyes, and what I saw
> Appear'd like something in myself, a dream,
> A prospect in my mind.

We can, I think, agree that both these passages are about a trancelike state, and that some words or phrases Wordsworth uses to describe that state are synonymous with, or related to, words and phrases in "A Slumber." Related to "slumber," for example, are "slept" in the first passage, and "a dream" in the second. We can parallel "she neither hears" in "A Slumber" with the "fleshly ear" that forgets its functions in the first passage; we can also parallel "nor sees" in "A Slumber" with the poet's forgetting that he had "bodily eyes" in the second. But notice this fact: in "A Slumber" these terms are used in a way precisely contrary to their use in the alleged parallels. According to Davies' reading of "A Slumber," it is the spirit that falls asleep—"A slumber did my *spirit* seal"—so that it neither hears nor sees. In the first passage, however, it is not the spirit, but what in the context is opposed to spirit—a physical sense, "the fleshly ear"—that sleeps. In the second passage, it is another physical sense, the "bodily eyes," that cease their ordinary function; and in both passages it is clearly implied that these lapses of normal functions in the bodily senses, instead of putting the spirit to sleep, are the conditions necessary to enable the spirit (or "soul") to come awake and function most fully. As Wordsworth put it succinctly in the poem "Tintern Abbey," in a passage Davies also cites as a parallel; in the trancelike state "we are laid asleep / In *body*, and become a living *soul*."

Take another of Davies' asserted parallels, cited from a draft that Wordsworth originally intended to include in *The Prelude*. The poet and a companion, on an evening walk, come suddenly upon a horse which "stood / Insensible and still."

> . . . breath, motion gone,
> Hairs, colour, all but shape and substance gone,
> Mane, ears, and tail, as lifeless as the trunk
> That had no stir of breath; we paused awhile
> In pleasure of the sight, and left him there
> With all his functions silently sealed up,
> Like an amphibious work of Nature's hand,
> A borderer dwelling betwixt life and death,
> A living Statue or a statued Life.

This marvelous passage, as Davies says, includes some equivalents to elements in "A Slumber": the total lack of motion, the functions that are "sealed up," the seeming imperviousness to time. There is, however, a serious difficulty with this parallel: these phrases don't describe a condition of the poet's spirit; they describe a horse. Of this fact Davies is naturally aware, but he nonetheless insists on the parallel by claiming that the "slumbering horse . . . can very reasonably be taken as . . . an 'objective correlative,' as an outward image for the inward experience" of the observer's slumber, or trancelike state. But the passage has no indication that the description of the horse is intended as a projected correlative of the observer's state of mind. In fact, the lines include an explicit description of the observer's state, and this is not in the least trancelike, but one of simple and passing pleasure at a visual perception: "we paused awhile / In pleasure of the sight."

This brings me to an objection to Davies' procedure throughout this part of his argument. To argue by parallels justly, one must not bias the selection, but adduce instances that are closest to the problematic poem in all relevant aspects; that is, not only in verbal similarities, but also in such features as literary genre, verse form, and length. Most of Davies' parallels, and all of the most telling ones, are descriptions of a trancelike state excerpted from Wordsworth's epic-length autobiographical poem, written in blank verse, *The Prelude*, or from the long blank-verse meditative poem "Tintern Abbey." The fact is, however, that with respect to the most salient features of "A Slumber," we can cite much closer parallels than those of Davies.

For example, "A Slumber" is a lyric poem, it is short, and it is written in ballad stanzas with alternating four- and three-foot iambic lines that rhyme a-b-a-b. In these generic and formal features, the near parallels are not blank-verse excerpts from *The Prelude*, but lyric poems by Wordsworth, and above all the four poems about the death of Lucy. Of these, three are short lyrics (from three to seven stanzas) and are written in the same ballad stanza as "A Slumber"—four- and three-foot iambic lines, rhyming a-b-a-b. To strengthen the case, various of the lyrics about Lucy include close verbal, imagistic, and semantic parallels to "A Slumber," if that poem is interpreted as an elegy—much closer parallels than any of those pointed to by Davies, if "A Slumber" is read as referring to the poet's entranced spirit.

To cite a single example: "Strange Fits of Passion" represents a lover riding toward Lucy's cottage, lulled by the steady beat of his horse's hoofs, and with his eyes fixed on the evening moon.

> In one of those sweet dreams, I slept,
> Kind Nature's gentlest boon!

The sleep and dream here have a function very like that in "A Slumber": they seal the lyric speaker's mind so that he is oblivious to "human fears"—that is, to the human awareness that all of those whom we love are vulnerable to death. This state of mind turns out to be illusory, yielding a security which, in each of the two poems, is falsified in the concluding stanza. Yet the metaphorical sleep of the spirit is, paradoxically, described as "Kind Nature's gentlest boon," for without it we would live in an unending anxiety about the mortal vulnerability of those we love. In "Strange Fits," as the narrator's horse plods along, the sinking moon, marking the passage of time, suddenly drops behind the cottage roof.

> What fond and wayward thoughts will slide
> > Into a Lover's head!
> "O mercy!" to myself I cried,
> > "If Lucy should be dead!"

But the position of this poem as one of a group of poems about Lucy reveals that this premonition of her death was neither fond (that is, "foolish") nor wayward, for it is validated by the grievous event. Similarly in "A Slumber" a girl, who to the lyric speaker's bemused spirit had seemed invulnerable to time, turns out to have been more vulnerable than the poet himself.

IV

The weight of the evidence has tipped decidedly to the standard reading of "A Slumber" (in which "she" in the third line refers to a girl), yet leaves Davies' reading (in which "she" refers to the poet's spirit) as an open, though greatly diminished possibility. We have an important remaining resource: to entertain each reading in turn as an hypothesis, in order to determine which one best fits the semantic aspects of the poem in its entirety. At once we discover the phenomenon of the hermeneutic circle. The semantic aspects of the language of "A Slumber" are not hard data, which decisively accord with or reject either of the hypothetical interpretations. They are soft data, malleable enough to adapt themselves to each of the two hypotheses, however divergent. Different potential ranges of significance in each component of the poem come into play, and fall into a different configuration, as we alter our interpretive vantage. In the first stanza, for example, that a slumber seals the speaker's spirit signifies, in the standard reading, that his spirit is lulled into forgetting its normal human fears that the one we love is fatally subject to time. In Davies' reading, the same verbal expression re-forms itself to signify that the poet's spirit, in its dreamlike trance, is oblivious to ordinary human anxieties, and is itself insensible to the passage of time. And so through the second stanza, we find adjustments in the meanings in each of the sequence of assertions, as we shift the reference of "she" from a girl to the speaker's spirit.

The situation of a reader who sets out to decide between the conflicting hypotheses, while difficult, is not desperate. The possible meanings of the phrasal elements of "A Slumber," although adaptive to each hypothesis, are not so malleable but that some elements resist one or the other interpretation, and cry out against too drastic a manipulation of its semantic possibilities— not with a public outcry, but within the sensibility of a qualified reader of an English lyric poem. Let's call such resistive elements "recalcitrancies"—verbal sequences which, to the semantic tact of a qualified reader, lie askew to, or go against the grain of, a particular interpretation.

I find several recalcitrancies in Davies' proposed reading. The pronoun "she" in the third line, given Wordsworth's usage in other poems, is amenable to serving as a reference to the noun "spirit," but manifests some unease in that function when "she" is repeated twice in the second stanza. And how plausible is it to claim that, even now, while he is in a trancelike state, the lyric speaker is able to describe that state of mind in such detail? Furthermore, what kind of sense does it make to assert that the tranced spirit has no motion or force of its own, but rolls round "with rocks and stones and trees"?

Admittedly, Davies can make shift with these recalcitrancies. He proposes, for example, that in the trancelike state of the poet's spirit, "the normal boundary between his own being and the rest of the world" disappears, so that he "*imagines* himself joined with the earth, and . . . identified with its diurnal motion." This, I confess, does make sense. But it makes sense only by pulling at what the expert reader, by his internalized norms of linguistic practice, intuits as the normal range of semantic possibilities, in order to nudge what lies athwart Davies' interpretation into alignment with it. There is, on the other hand, no recalcitrancy if we read the same words as referring to a girl who is in her grave, and so is entirely literally

> Rolled round in earth's diurnal course,
>   With rocks, and stones, and trees.

So throughout the poem, there are no recalcitrancies if we interpret "A Slumber" in the standard way. To be sure, the opening line—"A slumber did my spirit seal"—deviates markedly from colloquial English both in its word order and its high formality. But when we appraise the total poem, this deviation turns out to serve an important elegiac function—it is a ceremonial heightening of the style that imparts dignity, solemnity, and generality to the simple fact of the death of a single human being. From the first line to the last, "A Slumber" can be interpreted, without semantic strain, as an elegy about a girl who unexpectedly dies.

V

Taking into account all the evidence and counterevidence, which interpretation of Wordsworth's poem are we justified in choosing? Here we are confronted by another difficulty. The reasons for or against each reading are diverse, uncodified, and lacking in sharp criteria by which to measure their evidential weight. Furthermore, the diverse reasons are not only immeasurable; they are incommensurable with each other. How are we to judge the weight of a reason based on normal English grammar, or on Wordsworth's idiolect, against a reason based on more or less likely evidence that Wordsworth did, or did not, intend "A Slumber" to belong to a group of poems about Lucy; or both of these against an appeal to parallel passages in Wordsworth's other poems; and all of these to semantic recalcitrancies, or lack of them, in one or another of the two interpretations?

To put the matter in this way seems to make hopeless our attempt to achieve a valid interpretation of "A Slumber." As a matter of common practice, however, we are usually able to come to a firm decision about the purport of a poem. My procedure in this essay has been artificial, enforced by my disagreement with Hugh Sykes Davies. We normally interpret a poem not by reasoning about it, but by applying to it our interpretive tact, which is the seemingly intuitive product of all our prior engagements with poems. It is only when this intuition is challenged by a drastically divergent possibility that we feel the need to separate out, as explicit arguments, factors that are simultaneous and implicit in our tactful decisions. And after having assimilated the results of all the arguments pro and con, my interpretive tact finds Wordsworth's poem to be about a girl who unexpectedly dies.

We can bring to bear an additional argument; which is, that in the standard reading "A Slumber" is a much better poem than in Davies' reading. If the reasons I have cited were approximately in balance (though they are not), it would be reasonable—on the grounds that it would do the author the greater justice, and ourselves as readers a clear benefit—to choose the reading which yields the better poem. And I claim that, when read as an elegy, "A Slumber" has a much more effective dramatic structure, and achieves much greater emotional power, than when read as the exposition of a trance state of the speaker's spirit.

Davies' reading minimizes the significance of the sudden shift from the past tense in stanza 1 to the present tense in stanza 2. What we have, in his view, is the continuing description of a trancelike state that began then and continues now. In the standard reading, on the other hand, we experience the shocking revelation that a girl, who then seemed so vital as to allay any sense of her vulnerability to time, is now dead—she has died, as Paul de Man once put it, in the space between the two stanzas. Davies' reading also dissipates a powerful dramatic irony. Then, she had seemed "a thing" invulnerable to "earthly years"; now, the lyric speaker realizes that she has become a thing, rolled round, like rocks and stones and trees, in the revolution of the earth by which we measure earthly years. What we lose by Davies' reading is an austere representation of the awful suddenness, unexpectedness, and finality of death, set in the grand perspective of the astronomical processes of the natural world. We lose, that is, a major lyric instance of what the literary critic Walter Raleigh decades ago described as "Wordsworth's calm and almost terrible strength."

VI

As the upshot of all these considerations, I am confirmed in my assurance that the traditional interpretation of "A Slumber" is correct. But I am confronted by a disconcerting discovery. Certain though I am that the traditional reading is right and Davies' reading is wrong, I find that some of the graduate students in the seminar I described disagree with me; that my fellow director of the seminar, Max Black, disagrees with me; and that several of my literary friends also disagree with me.

What to do when, myself so certain, I am confronted by a contrary judgment by indubitably qualified readers? My first and very human impulse is to get angry. But I resist the impulse, and run again through all the reasons for my interpretation that I have formulated. When I have done this, I can do no more; I have reached the point in giving reasons at which, as the philosopher Wittgenstein put it, "the spade turns." If a qualified reader of lyric poems stubbornly holds to a contradictory reading, I can only wait, with what patience I can muster, for an infusion of grace—an interpretive conversion—that will get the reader to see what to me is so evident. But upon considering the matter, I realize that such a reader feels the same way about my stubbornness in maintaining my interpretation. So I have to admit that in this, and in similar instances of interpretive deadlock, some qualified readers' certainty will be contradicted by the certainty of other qualified readers. And by this admission, I seem to have reasoned myself into sharing the skepticism I set out to disprove: that in interpreting poems, no reading can claim to be the right reading.

At this juncture, I find illuminating observations by Ludwig Wittgenstein, which I venture to summarize in this way: Our uses of language are inter-involved with "forms of life"—activities which incorporate a diversity of language games that have been formed to accomplish a diversity of human purposes. Each language game operates according to a set of rules, some of which may overlap with the rules of other language games, while others are specific to its particular enterprise. In consequence of the differences in their rules, although a number of language games undertake to achieve certainty, Wittgenstein points out, "the kind of certainty is the kind of language-game."[2]

It is certain, for example, that "ten divided by five equals two." It is also certain that Newton's laws of motion are valid. Certainty in the language game of mathematics, however, and certainty in that of physical science depend on the application of rules specific to each. The two language games nonetheless have a common feature: both are highly specialized, designed systematically to exclude any role by individual human differences, in order to achieve universal agreement among all those who are competent players in each game.

The language game in the enterprise we call literary criticism, on the other hand, is specifically organized to allow room for the play of individual human differences. Always readers bring to bear on the interpretation of a poem diverse sensibilities, ranges of experience, and individual temperaments. The consequence is that in some interpretive judgments, one's certainty about an interpretation, however supported by valid reasons, will remain open to disagreement by other qualified readers. The interpretation of the basic reference of Wordsworth's "A Slumber" falls into this category.

It should be added that in this openness to disagreement consists the validity, as well as the vitality and enduring interest, of literary criticism. The inevitability of disagreement in this, as in many other humanistic pursuits, rests on a basic value: the rich diversity of individual human beings. The way of wisdom is to proceed rationally, to strive for a maximum consensus, and—when all possible evidence is adduced to no avail—to agree to disagree, in the recognition that some disagreements in basic humanistic enterprises are ultimately unresolvable.

VII

There remains another interpretive maneuver—one that is confidently to be expected in the climate of critical opinion inaugurated by William Empson's greatly influential *Seven Types of Ambiguity*, published in 1930. By "ambiguity" Empson signifies multiple meanings, and he proposes that in many instances in which critics contest the interpretation of a poetic passage, the either/or should be converted into a both-and. A few seminar students suggested that we ought to read "A Slumber" as referring both to a girl and to the poet's spirit. The English critic A. P. Rossiter proposed in 1961 that in "A Slumber" the question "Which is right, A or B, is a non-question: the poem is ambivalent," and "is only fully experienced when both opposites are held and included in a 'two-eyed' view."[3] And in 1984, twelve years after our joint seminar, Max Black published an essay in which he maintained that Wordsworth's poem "must be regarded as an irreducible case of radical ambiguity," in which both readings are equally valid.[4]

I find a number of Empson's examples of multiple meanings convincing, and have published essays in which I interpret some poetic passages as variously and simultaneously meaningful. For example, in the concluding scene of Shakespeare's *Antony and Cleopatra*, when Cleopatra puts the asp to her breast, what she says is richly multiplex in meaning:

> Come, thou mortal wretch,
> With thy sharp teeth this knot intrinsicate

> Of life at once untie. Poor venomous fool,
> Be angry, and dispatch.

The "mortal wretch," the asp, is at once death-dealing and itself subject to death. "Wretch" and "fool" express both contempt and pity—she goes on to refer to the asp as "my baby at my breast, / That sucks the nurse asleep." The adjective "intrinsicate" may be read as blending "intrinsic" (the knot is inescapably part of life) and "intricate." Also, two diverse meanings of "dispatch," "make haste" and "kill," are equally and simultaneously relevant. There is however, a necessary condition for this and other instances of multiple significance: the meanings, no matter how diverse, must be mutually compatible. And in Wordsworth's "A Slumber," the two contested meanings are drastically incompatible.

On this issue it is useful to consider Wittgenstein's famed example of the duck-rabbit.[5] He presents a simple linear outline. You look at it and see a duck. You look again, and see a rabbit. You cannot, however, see the drawing simultaneously as both a duck and a rabbit.

Similarly, in reading "A Slumber" I can read "she" in the third line, and in the statements that follow, as referring either to a girl or to the poet's spirit, but I cannot read these pronouns as referring simultaneously both to a girl and to the poet's spirit. The two interpretations can only be read as sequential alternatives; but to read it in this alternating fashion trivializes Wordsworth's poem, converting it into a puzzle-poem, a complex linguistic trick in which you see first this, then that: now it's a duck, now a rabbit; now it's about a girl, now about the poet's spirit. The only way to salvage Wordsworth's great lyric is to read it as solely about a girl who unexpectedly dies. That is the correct interpretation. The alternative interpretation, that it is about the poet's spirit, is a misreading, and should be rejected.

VIII

In closing his essay Hugh Sykes Davies remarks, disarmingly, that he does not "believe that the whole train of argument presented here in favour of the new interpretation is decisive. It does, however, seem enough . . . to deserve a run for its money." But as the apostle Paul said, "Know ye not that they which run in a race run all, but only one receiveth the prize?" Davies has run a very good race; but mindful of Wittgenstein's insight that the kind of certainty is the kind of language game, I assert without hesitation that his interpretation of "A Slumber" is certainly wrong.

NOTES

1. Hugh Sykes Davies, "Another New Poem by Wordsworth," *Essays in Criticism* 15 (1965): 135–61.
2. Ludwig Wittgenstein, *Philosophical Investigations*, translated by G. E. M. Anscombe (Oxford, 1953), pp. 224–26.
3. A. P. Rossiter, *Angels with Horns* (New York, 1961).
4. Max Black, "The Radical Ambiguity of a Poem," *Synthèse* 59 (April 1984): 89–107.
5. Wittgenstein, *Philosophical Investigations*, pp. 194–99.

"This Green Earth": The Vision of Nature in the Romantic Poets

I.

"THIS GREEN EARTH." Wordsworth used the phrase in his early poem "Tintern Abbey," and repeated it no less than eight times in his other poems. I have appropriated it as an apt identifier for my topic today: the way that many major Romantic poets envisioned "nature," in the basic denotation of the term—that is, everything on earth other than human beings and the results of human handiwork.

Romantic poets, at the turn of the nineteenth century, introduced into the literary realm an extraordinary emphasis on the natural world, and an unprecedented set of concepts, attitudes, and feelings with reference to that world. Wordsworth's "Tintern Abbey," which he composed in 1798 at the age of twenty-eight, formulated and helped to establish a vision of nature that is distinctively Romantic. That is, the poem manifests a sense of total affinity and communion with the natural world by representing it as a living entity in whose life—Coleridge as well as Wordsworth sometimes called it "the one life"—all things, human and nonhuman, participate. As Coleridge later put it in "The Eolian Harp" (1817):

> O the one Life, within us and abroad,
> Which meets all Motion and becomes its soul . . .
> Rhythm in all thought, and joyance everywhere.

"Tintern Abbey" also exemplifies what is sometimes called the Romantic "religion of nature," for it transfers to this green earth attributes, together with the appropriate feelings of reverence and awe, that in earlier eras of Western culture had been applied exclusively to God.

I want to emphasize that the Romantic vision of the natural world is not an outmoded phenomenon, of no more than historical interest. The Romantic attitudes toward nature are in fact of crucial import to us, because relevant to pressing contemporary concerns. That relevance becomes evident if we substitute for the term "nature" the current term "environment," and if we substitute for the Romantic concept of the one life, in which human beings are interrelated with all that is nonhuman, the current concept of "ecology"—the interrelations and interdependence of all living beings with each other and with the physical environment.

We know today that our physical and biological environment is under severe stress. We are polluting our soil, water, and air. We are rapidly depleting this green earth of its greenery, its forests and plains. We are exterminating, at an increasing pace, plant and animal species which, once lost, can never be reconstituted. And at a frightening rate we are overpopulating our crowded earth. We—or at least many of us—know these things, from what ecological scientists tell us and from personal observation. But simply to *know* such things, on the intellectual level, is not enough, as the Romantic poet Shelley pointed out so early as 1821 in his essay *A Defence of Poetry*. "There is no want of knowledge," Shelley wrote, "respecting what is wisest and best in morals, government, and political economy." And about the natural sciences and their practical applications, he said: "The cultivation of those sciences which have enlarged the limits of the empire of man over the external world has, for want of the poetical faculty [the imagination], circumscribed those of the internal world, and man, having enslaved the elements, remains himself a slave." What we lack, Shelley said, is

> the creative faculty to imagine that which we know, we want the generous impulse to act that which we imagine, we want the poetry of life.

For, he declares, it is especially poetry—defined broadly as any "expression of the Imagination"—that "compels us to feel that which we perceive, and to imagine that which we know."

I shall try to specify some of the chief ways in which poets of the Romantic era (the quarter-century beginning in the late 1790s) imagined what they knew about their physical environment. To stay within the limits of your patience, I have to be very selective. I'll focus mainly on English poets, although what they say holds true for a number of poets in Germany as well; while among the English examples I'll attend mainly to two major poets of the first Romantic generation: William Wordsworth, born 1770, and Samuel Coleridge, born 1772. And even from these writers, I have time only to select a few passages to represent the diverse ways in which they expressed a hitherto unexampled set of attitudes and feelings toward the green earth and the forms of life that inhabit it.

In part, the Romantic representations of nature were a reaction against the products of the industrial revolution during the preceding half-century—the age of iron and steam, of the factory system (in the phrase of the Romantic poet William Blake, "the dark Satanic mills"), and of the sprawling urbanization that were making conspicuous and ugly inroads (again in a phrase from Blake) on "England's green and pleasant land." For example, Wordsworth's epoch-marking poem that we call, for short, "Tintern Abbey," was written, as the full title specifies, while he contemplated the natural scene from the banks of the river Wye "a few miles above Tintern Abbey." As Wordsworth knew, the river a few miles *below* Tintern Abbey, to cite a popular guidebook of the time by William Gilpin, was "full of shipping, carrying coal and timber"; there were also along the banks of the river iron-manufacturing furnaces that made the water "ouzy, and discolored" in the tidal section downstream. And some fifteen years after "Tintern Abbey," in the eighth book of his long poem *The Excursion* (1814), Wordsworth vehemently attacked what he called the "outrage done to nature" by factories and "the manufacturing spirit," as well as by the expanding manufacturing towns, with the result, he laments, that one sees "the barren wilderness erased, / Or disappearing."

In great part, however, the Romantic vision of nature was in vehement reaction against the post-Newtonian and post-Cartesian world-view prevalent among the philosophers and intellectuals of the eighteenth-century Enlightenment. Newton's science had postulated a universe in which the ultimate elements are particles of matter in motion—for the very good reason that these are things that can be numbered and measured, and thus are capable of being managed mathematically. But later thinkers, building on some passages in Newton's own speculations, had converted these scientific postulates from a conceptual model into a world-picture; that is, into the representation of the way, deep down, things really are. S. T. Coleridge, for example, who was a metaphysician as well as a poet, greatly admired what he called "the immortal Newton" as a theoretical and experimental physicist; he decried, however, the conversion of Newton's postulate of particles in motion from what he called "a fiction of science" into "a truth of fact," thereby making this vital world into "a lifeless Machine whirled about by the dust of its own grinding" ("Conclusion" to *Aids to Reflection*). Equally intolerable to the Romantic sensibility was the dualism of the reigning philosophy and psychology of the preceding century, which established an absolute division between the human mind, or "subject," and its material physical milieu, and so replaced the concrete, vital, and companionable world of traditional European culture with a world consisting, fundamentally, of particles in purposeless motion, connected by purely causal relationships.

From such a representation of the world both Romantic philosophers and Romantic poets recoiled with repulsion and disbelief. Typical is the response of the young Goethe and his friends to the Baron d'Holbach's *System of Nature* (1770), a book that undertook to reduce the phenomenal world—and also human consciousness and purposiveness—to the operation of causal laws on material particles. This book, Goethe wrote, "appeared to us so dark, so Cimmerian, so deathlike, that we found it difficult to endure its presence, and shuddered at it as at a specter."

> How hollow and empty did we feel in this melancholy, atheistical half-night, in which earth vanished with all its images, heaven with all its stars. There was to be an eternal matter in eternal motion, and by this motion, right and left and in all directions, without anything further, were to be produced the infinite phenomena of existence.
>
> (*Dichtung und Wahreit*, Part III, Book xi)

Similarly repelled, Coleridge, in his periodical *The Friend*, described the predominant world-view of the preceding century as "that intuition of things" in which "we think of ourselves as separated beings, and place nature in antithesis to the mind as object to subject, thing to thought, death to life." And as he wrote to Wordsworth in May of 1815, "the philosophy of mechanism . . . in every thing that is most worthy of the human intellect strikes *Death*." Wordsworth agreed that the philosophical separation of mind from nature is lethal; as he wrote in a manuscript version of "The Ruined Cottage," 1797–98: "solitary objects . . . beheld / In disconnection are dead and spiritless," as opposed to the unifying vision in which "all things shall live in us and we shall live / In all things that surround us."

To many Romantic writers, the theory world posited by philosophical mechanism and dualism was not only intolerable to human needs, but drastically incompatible with ordinary human experience. The central enterprise of the philosophical systems of Schelling, Hegel, and other German thinkers was to reunite the "subject and object"—or in their alternate terms, "ego and non-ego," "spirit and the other," "mind and nature"—that Descartes and post-Cartesian philosophers had put asunder; they would thus restore to the lived world its sensuous concreteness and human values, and thereby make it possible for human beings to feel that they belonged again in a world from which—in a term Hegel established to define the basic human malaise—in a world from which they have been *"entfremdet"*—"alienated."

For early Romantic poets as for contemporary philosophers, a cardinal enterprise was to heal the breach that culture had imposed between subject and object, between the self and the natural world, so as to revivify and rehumanize the world and make it adequate to human experience and responsive to human needs. In an essay "On Poesy or Art," S. T. Coleridge elaborated the views of the German philosopher F. S. Schelling, in a statement that serves to identify what is most distinctive in the literature of his time. Poetry or art, he says, is the mediatress between, the reconciler of nature and man. It is, therefore, the power of humanizing nature, of infusing the thoughts and passions of man into every thing which is the object of his contemplation. . . . To make the external internal, the internal external, to make nature thought, and thought nature,—this is the mystery of genius in the Fine Arts.

II.

In reaction against the bleak theory world of mechanism and dualism, Romantic poets achieved intellectual and emotional relationships to the natural world unexampled in earlier cultural history. To formulate these experiences in words, they did not invent new terms; instead, they enlarged the expressive possibilities of the existing vocabulary by inventing types of metaphor that would make the old vocabulary adequate to express the new states of consciousness. Let me present several passages, to indicate how early Romantic poets developed metaphors that, as Coleridge put it, would humanize nature, and serve to "make the external internal, the internal external, to make nature thought, and thought nature."

My first instance is from Wordsworth's great narrative poem, "The Ruined Cottage," which he composed in 1797–98 but left in manuscript. Wordsworth describes an eight-year-old shepherd boy—patently modeled on his own young self—who from a mountaintop sees the sun "rise up and bathe the world in light."

> He looked,
> The ocean and the earth beneath him lay
> In gladness and deep joy. The clouds were touched
> And in their silent faces did he read

Unutterable love. Sound needed none
Nor any voice of joy: his spirit drank
The spectacle. Sensation, soul and form
All melted into him. They swallowed up
His animal being; in them did he live
And by them did he live. They were his life.

Here we have the paradigmatic Wordsworthian—and widely Romantic—situation: a human being, solitary, confronts a scene ("He *looked*"), and the interaction between the viewer and the scene, the subject and the object, generates the poetic passage. Now, note Wordsworth's metaphors for this interaction. The observer's spirit "drank / The spectacle"; that is, the observer ingested the objects of the natural world, so that these, in another metaphor, "melted into him," and thus became part of his identity. Note in addition that the metaphoric process goes two ways: as the observer "drank" the spectacle, so the objects in that spectacle "swallowed up" his animal being. The observer, having ingested the scene, is in turn ingested by it; in Coleridge's terms, the observer, having internalized the external, is then himself internalized. The result of this mutual appropriation is the interfusion of outer and inner, of the human self and the natural world, into one being: "They were his life." And this visionary condition, in which Wordsworth expresses the one life not as a concept but as a moment of experience, is signalized by an enraptured state of mind that Wordsworth twice calls "joy."

Metaphors of ingestion, especially drinking, occur repeatedly in Wordsworth's descriptions of the interpenetration, through the senses, of mind and nature. One example is Wordsworth's representation, in *The Prelude*, of what he calls "a Spot of Time"; that is, a visionary moment of perception of the outer world, by which, as Wordsworth puts it in another of his ingestive metaphors, "our minds / Are nourished and invisibly repaired."

> And afterwards the wind and sleety rain,
> And all the business of the elements,
> The single sheep, and the one blasted tree,
> And the bleak music of that old stone wall,
> The noise of wood and water . . .
> All these were spectacles and sounds to which
> I often would repair, and thence would drink
> As at a fountain.

Wordsworth exploits a variety of other metaphors to express the integration of the external with the internal, of the human with the nonhuman. As a prime example, here is a passage, drafted in 1799, that Wordsworth later reworked for inclusion in his poetic autobiography, *The Prelude* (1805). As a boy, he mimicked the hooting of owls that they might answer him.

> But at times they did not answer.
> Then often in that silence, while I hung
> Listening, a sudden shock of mild surprize
> Would carry far into my heart the voice
> Of mountain torrents; or the visible scene
> Would enter unawares into my mind
> With all its solemn imagery, its rocks,
> Its woods, and that uncertain heaven received
> Into the bosom of the steady lake.

Of this passage, Coleridge remarked: "Had I met these lines running wild in the desert of Arabia, I should have instantly screamed out, 'Wordsworth!'" Why are these lines unmistakably Wordsworthian?

Note that by the phrase "far into my heart" Wordsworth attributes to the mind, metaphorically, the spatial dimension of depth—a space into which the sound of torrents is carried, and into which "the visible scene" can "enter" and be internalized. At the same time, outer objects are unobtrusively humanized. The torrents are given, metaphorically, a human feature, a "voice"; and to the lake is attributed another human feature, a maternal "bosom," into which it receives, comfortingly, the "uncertain heaven"—that is, the shimmering reflection of the sky in the still water of the lake. In a final stroke of invention, Wordsworth annuls the division between mind and nature by tacitly equating the mind's perception of the outer scene with the outer scene's reception of the objects that it reflects. That is, in the same way that the lake receives the rocks, woods, and uncertain heaven, so the mind receives the lake, including its reflected imagery of rocks, woods, and the uncertain heaven. Inner and outer, human and nonhuman, mind and nature are merged, metaphorically, into a seamless unity.

I have time for one other example, related to the closing lines of the passage I have just quoted, that ascribes to the lake a comforting maternal bosom. In the second book of *The Prelude*, Wordsworth struggles to invent a vocabulary—inescapably, a metaphoric vocabulary—in the attempt to say what no one, so far as I know, had said before. Wordsworth's point is that a world that an infant gets to know while in the security of his mother's arms, and while nursing at his mother's breast, is a world transformed:

> Blest the infant Babe . . .
> Nursed in his mother's arms, who sinks to sleep
> Rocked on his Mother's breast; who with his soul
> Drinks in the feelings of his Mother's eye!
> For him, in one dear Presence, there exists
> A virtue which irradiates and exalts
> Objects through widest intercourse of sense.
> No outcast he, bewildered and depressed:

> Along his infant veins are interfused
> The gravitation and the filial bond
> Of nature that connect him with the world.

In these circumstances, a world that would otherwise be an alien object is experienced (in Wordsworth's figure) as irradiated by human feelings, with the result that the infant is bound doubly to the world—he is bound physically, by the pull of gravity, and emotionally, by a transference to the world of the loving interrelations between mother and son. In Wordsworth's terse phrasing: "No outcast he," for

> Along his infant veins are interfused
> The gravitation and the filial bond
> Of nature that connect him with the world.

As in these examples, so elsewhere in Wordsworth's early poetry, natural objects are metaphorically received, enter, flow into, sink down, and melt into the mind, while the mind dwells on, drinks, feeds upon, and conducts emotional interchanges with natural objects. The division between what is external and internal thus dissipates, transforming a divorced and alien world, in which the human being would feel himself to be outcast, into a congenial world, in which he can feel thoroughly at home.

III.

The need to be at home again in the world—that is a persistent motif in Romantic literature, and in Romantic philosophy as well. A widespread structural trope, shared by poets and philosophers, figures human life as a circuitous journey away from home, through an estranged world, in an irremissive but unknowing quest for the home that has been left behind. Wordsworth's auto-biographical poem *The Prelude* is structured as a laborious spiritual journey which, at its end, turns out to be preliminary to another poem which has been the unrecognized goal of the author's spiritual quest from the beginning; that goal, as the title of the following poem specifies, is home—*Home at Grasmere*. Hegel's exactly contemporaneous philosophical work, *Phenomenology of the Spirit*, turns out to have the same plot. It represents the evolving vicissitudes of the Universal Spirit in its self-educative journey through history, starting with its departure from its own alienated self, around and up and back, toward the culmination in which it will repossess its alienated self, and so find itself, in Hegel's phrase, *"bei sich"*—"at home with itself in its otherness." As the poet Novalis described this dominant philosophical trope of his era: "Philosophy is really homesickness—the compulsion to be everywhere at home [*Trieb überall zu Hause zu sein*]."

I want to glance at Coleridge's "The Rime of the Ancient Mariner" to show how all strands of the great Romantic theme—the circular journey through alienation back to integration, involving the recognition of the one shared life and the realization of what it means to be at home again in a world from which we have been estranged—are incorporated in the plot of the best-known narrative poem in English. The mariner departs from his native land and sails toward the Antarctic. In a desolate icy setting, a lone albatross appears. The sailors hail it "as if it had been a Christian soul," and in the ancient ritual of welcoming a human traveler, give it food. Suddenly the mariner, "in contempt of the laws of hospitality," as Coleridge's marginal gloss specifies, kills the albatross with his crossbow. This seemingly gratuitous act expresses the condition of the mariner's spirit: his prideful self-sufficiency, his readiness to sever himself from a universal community, the fellow participants in a shared life. The mariner's punishment, as the ship moves north in the Pacific Ocean toward the equator, is to experience the full measure of the isolation he has elected—his fellow sailors fall dead, and he finds himself becalmed in a dead and static nature that has become alien and inimical to him:

> Alone, alone, all, all alone
> Alone on a wide, wide sea.

The only living things he sees are the water-snakes on a rotting sea—"only a thousand thousand slimy things / Lived on, and so did I." As Coleridge's marginal gloss explains, "He despiseth the creatures of the calm."

At this lowest point of total stasis comes the narrative reversal, announced in the lines, "The moving Moon went up the sky, / And nowhere did abide." Coleridge's matchless prose gloss on these lines is designed to make clear to the reader what the mariner, by suffering alienation and solitude, has learned. The mariner humanizes the motions of the moon and stars; and the insistent repetitions in his interpretation of their circular courses reveals how profoundly he has learned what it means to belong—to belong to a place, a native land, a family, a home:

> In his loneliness and fixedness he yearneth towards the journeying moon, and the stars that still sojourn, yet still move onward; and everywhere the blue sky belongs to them, and is their appointed rest, and their native country and their own natural homes, which they enter unannounced, as lords that are certainly expected and yet there is a silent joy at their arrival.

The lesson of community thus achieved, the mariner looks again at the water snakes; but what he had earlier seen as loathsome, he now sees to be beautiful, and to be joying in the life they share with their penitent observer; and in an unpremeditated burst of familial love, he blesses them:

O happy living things! no tongue
Their beauty might declare
A spring of love gushed from my heart,
And I blessed them unaware.

At once the terrible spell snaps; the dead elements of nature "burst into life" and move the mariner to complete the circle of his spiritual journey. In literal geographic fact, he completes his circumnavigation of the globe, to end his voyage at the precise place where it had begun. But only now, after the alienation he has deserved and suffered, does he become aware of what it means to be at home in what the gloss specifies as "his native country."

Oh! dream of joy! is this indeed
The light-house top I see?
Is this the hill? Is this the kirk?
Is this mine own countree?

IV.

To be estranged from the natural world was to Coleridge, as to fellow Romantics, the radical affliction of the human condition; it is to experience as a lived reality what he regarded as the post-Newtonian world-view, "the intuition" in which, as he wrote in *The Friend*, we "place nature in antithesis to the mind, as . . . death to life." To such a view Coleridge opposed that alternative "intuition of things which arises when we possess ourselves, as one with the whole." This is the condition in which alienation is annulled, and the human individual breaks through the barrier of self to achieve awareness of the one life that he shares with all living beings, and with all nature. And of this intuition the emotional accompaniment is what Coleridge—in what for him, as for many of his contemporaries is a specialized term— calls "joy" or "joyance." As Coleridge put it in his *Philosophical Lectures*:

> In joy individuality is lost. . . . To have a genius is to live in the universal, to know no self but that which is reflected not only from the faces of all around us, our fellow creatures, but reflected from the flowers, the trees, the beasts, yea from the very surface of the [waters and the] sands of the desert.

Repeatedly in other Romantic writers we find the acme of human experience represented as a breakthrough to a joyous participation with the abundant diversity of all living species. William Blake, in his buoyant middle thirties, wrote of the renewal of "the fiery joy":

> For everything that lives is holy, life delights in life;
> Because the soul of sweet delight can never be defil'd.

In Night the ninth of his *Four Zoas*, Blake represents mankind's climactic recognition that outer nature is no other than his own estranged self—Blake's equivalent in myth of Hegel's philosophy of alienation and reintegration—as an exuberant celebration of the rebirth of a dead and wintry world:

> For Lo the winter melted away upon the distant hills
> And all the black mould sings. She speaks to her infant race, her milk
> Descends down on the sand. . . .
> The roots shoot thick thro the solid rocks bursting their way
> They cry out in joys of existence. . . .

> The bats burst forth from the hardened slime crying
> To one another, What are we & whence is our joy and
> delight?

Twice in this passage the apocalypse of the imagination is signalized by the term "joy." We don't think of Wordsworth as an exuberant poet, yet his elation equals Blake's at moments of imaginative insight when, as he says in the eighth book of *The Prelude*, "The pulse of Being everywhere was felt . . . / One galaxy of life and joy." Hence, in the second book of *The Prelude*, his exultant response, again called "joy," to his achieved sense that he participates in the plenitude and diversity of the one life, whether on land, in the air, or within the depths of the sea:

> I was only then
> Contented when with bliss ineffable
> I felt the sentiment of Being spread
> O'er all that leaps, and runs, and shouts, and sings,
> Or beats the gladsome air; o'er all that glides
> Beneath the wave, yea, in the wave itself,
> And mighty depth of waters. Wonder not
> If such my transports were, for in all things
> I saw one life, and felt that it was joy.

As a reminder that the Romantic vision of nature was voiced by German as well as by English writers, I shall cite a passage by the poet Friedrich Hölderlin. In the 1790s the young Hölderlin wrote a romance in prose, entitled *Hyperion*, of which the plot, as he summarizes it in his "Preface," reiterates the central Romantic theme of the basic human need to reintegrate with an alienated nature.

To end that eternal conflict between our self and the world
. . . to unite ourselves with nature so as to form one endless
whole—that is the goal of all our striving.

In the course of the narrative, the protagonist momentarily
reaches this goal, in an achievement of unison with the vigor and
variousness of life in the natural world. Although in prose instead
of verse, Hölderlin's rapturous expression of such an imaginative
moment is remarkably close to that of Wordsworth:

> Each living thing flew and leaped and struggled out into the
> divine air, and beetles and swallows and doves and storks
> wheeled and mingled in joyous confusion in the depths and
> heights, and the steps of those who were bound to earth turned
> into flight; over the furrows charged the horse and over the
> hedges the roe, and out of the depths of the sea the fish rose
> and leaped over its surface.
>
> So didst thou lie poured forth, sweet Life. . . .

I have time for only one other example of the Romantic celebration of the sense of the one shared life. It is from Shelley's
great elegy, "Adonais," composed in the Italian springtime of 1821.
The poem memorializes the death of young John Keats, and concludes with a death wish by Shelley himself; yet in the course of
the poem, the poet responds to the upsurge of life in the spring,
and to the joyous urgency in all living things to procreate more
life, in a rapture that outsoars even his Romantic contemporaries.
Here Shelley comes close to the expressive limits of language, yet
without strain, despite the stringencies in meter and rhyme of the
complex Spenserian stanza.

"Ah woe is me!" The passage begins with the classical cry of
elegiac mourning, and proceeds to an equally traditional *topos*—
introduced into the pastoral elegy by Theocritus, more than two

thousand years earlier—which laments the finality of human death in contrast to the rebirth of the natural world in spring. But in Shelley, the ancient commonplace triggers an ecstatic realization of a teeming universal life:

> The amorous birds now pair in every brake,
> And build their mossy homes in field and brere;
> And the green lizard, and the golden snake,
> Like unimprisoned flames, out of their trance awake.

Now, the Shelleyan liftoff:

> Through wood and stream and field and hill and Ocean
> A quickening life from the Earth's heart has burst
> As it has ever done, with change and motion,
> From the great morning of the world when first
> God dawned on Chaos; in its stream immersed
> All baser things pant with life's sacred thirst;
> Diffuse themselves, and spend in love's delight,
> The beauty and the joy of their renewed might.

V.

Some version of cosmic ecology—the sense of close affinity between the human and the natural world, and of joyous participation in their shared life—is to be found in later writers who, in this aspect, are recognizably in the Romantic lineage. I shall cite three instances, two English and one American.

The first is D. H. Lawrence, who put forward the Romantic concept of alienation and reintegration in its uncompromisingly primitive form; that is, in the mythical mode of the One Primal Man who has fallen into division, but yearns to be reunified with his estranged natural self. In his book entitled *Apocalypse*, written in 1932, Lawrence announced: "We and the cosmos are one. The cosmos is a vast living body, of which we are still parts. . . . Now all this is *literally* true, as men knew in the great past, and as they will know again." The development of human self-consciousness and the expansion of abstract knowledge gradually divided this cosmos, in a process that reached a crisis in the sixteenth and seventeenth centuries, when the scientific world-view "substituted the non-vital universe of forces and mechanistic order . . . and the long slow death of the human being set in." Lawrence continues, in his haunting rhetoric:

> What man most passionately wants is his living wholeness and his living unison. . . . I am part of the sun as my eye is part of me. That I am part of the earth my feet know perfectly, and my blood is part of the sea. . . .
> What we want is to . . . re-establish the living organic connections, with the cosmos, the sun and earth, with mankind and nation and family. Start with the sun, and the rest will slowly, slowly happen.

My next reference is the opening stanza of a poem by Dylan Thomas, composed in 1933, "The force that through the green fuse." (The "green fuse" is the hollow stem of a plant.) Note the interchanges of "green" and "wintry," which are literal for the natural plant and season but metaphorical for human beings, and of "fever," which is literal for human beings but metaphorical for a plant:

> The force that through the green fuse drives the flower
> Drives my green age; that blasts the roots of trees
> Is my destroyer.
> And I am dumb to tell the crooked rose
> My youth is bent by the same wintry fever.

The metaphoric interplay between the human and the nonhuman, between the internal and the external, is recognizably Wordsworthian, although the voice is unmistakably that of Dylan Thomas. The poetic voices both of Wordsworth and of Thomas are remote from that of A. R. Ammons, who wrote free verse in the American vernacular, and with the rhythms of everyday conversation. We nonetheless recognize in Ammons' nature poems—"Mansion" is an example—his expression of a Romantic sense of commonality with the life and death of all natural things, on the earth from which all originate, and to which all return. The poem named "Still" records Ammons' sudden accession to a state of consciousness that Romantic writers called "joy," the ecstatic awareness that the self is inter-involved with the natural world in one all-inclusive life:

> everything is
> magnificent with existence, is in
> surfeit of glory. . . .
> I whirled through transfigurations up and down,
> transfigurations of size and shape and place:
>> at one sudden point came still,
>> stood in wonder:
> moss, beggar, weed, tick, pine, self, magnificent
>> with being!

Whatever the difference in its linguistic register, the similarity of this passage is patent to Wordsworth's expression of "bliss ineffable" when he "felt the sentiment of Being, spread / O'er all that moves, and all that seemeth still." And Ammons' short poem entitled "Reflective" is recognizably, although in a whimsical rendering, a Wordsworthian recognition of kinship with even so lowly a being as a common weed:

I found a
weed
that had a

mirror in it
and that
mirror

looked in at
a mirror
in

me that
had a
weed in it.

COLERIDGE AND HIS philosophical contemporaries, as we have
seen, claimed that the alienation of humanity from nature "strikes
death." Science and the technology it fosters, when applied heedlessly or with unbridled greed, has turned Coleridge's metaphoric
death of nature into a grimly literal possibility. Many scientists
and ecologists have recently taken the lead in trying to persuade
us, by an appeal to the facts, of this lethal threat to the natural
world. It remains to be seen whether merely to know the facts
is enough, or whether it will take a revival and dissemination
of some equivalent to the Romantic vision of nature to enable
us, in Shelley's great phrase, "to imagine that which we know."
It seems likely that only such a motive power—such an *emotive* power—will suffice to release the energies, the invention,
and the will to make the sacrifices that are needed if we are to
salvage this no-longer-quite-so-green earth while it is still fit
to live on.

Kant and the Theology of Art

———

M Y CONCERN IS with the origin, and with the antecedents in intellectual history, of the modern theory
of art-as-such. I use "art-as-such" as a convenient
shorthand for the following views:

1. All works of "fine art," whether a painting, a poem, sculpture,
music, or architecture, can be defined in a way that demarcates
them from all other human products, by reference to distinctive
features in the experience of the perceiver, or else by reference to
distinctive attributes of the works themselves. Usually it is assumed
that the normative aesthetic experience and the defining attributes
of the work of art are mutually implicative, or at least correlative.

2. In terms of the perceiver's experience, a work of art is said to be
contemplated, and to be contemplated disinterestedly. This claim

From *Notre Dame English Journal* 13 (1981). Reprinted by permission of the
publisher.

signifies that the work is attended to absorbedly and exclusively, without reference to anything beyond its own bounds, and for its own sake—that is, independently of personal concerns or desires, and without regard to its referential truth, or its pleasurable or emotional effects, or its practical use, or its moral content or implications. A work of art may or may not be true to life or the world, or serve useful or pleasurable or emotional ends, or have moral effects; but consideration of such matters is held to be irrelevant, or even destructive, to the purely disinterested contemplation of the work as such, simply as a work of art.

3. In terms of its own attributes, the work of art is said to be an object which is self-sufficient, nonreferential, "autotelic," autonomous, and independent of relations to anything outside its own bounds. Alternatively, it is said to be an end in itself, not a means to an end beyond itself; or else its end is asserted to be internal, not external, and its artistic value to be intrinsic, not extrinsic. The work, then, is conceived as an entity of which the end is simply to exist, to be what it is for our disinterested contemplation.

These are to us thoroughly familiar terms and assertions. They constitute—in various formulations, and with varying emphasis on the percipient's experience of art as such, or on the attributes of the work as such—an area of congruence among New Critics, Chicago Aristotelians, American contextual critics, and Continental formalists. The claim that a literary text is not mimetic, expressive, or pragmatic, but a self-sustaining system that generates its own meanings and purely internal relations, is basic to modern structuralism. The kinds of assertions I have cited are also central to most modern theories of aesthetics and philosophies of art; even theorists who dissent from some aspect of this view usually define their negative position by reference to these assertions as the prevailing ones. To many of us, such assertions also seem to be patent truths, confirmed by our ordinary experience of works of art. The historical facts, however, should give us pause. For some two thousand years of theoretical concern with these matters, it occurred to no thinker to claim that a human artifact is to be contemplated disinterestedly, for its own sake, as its own end and for its internal values, without reference to things, human beings, purposes, or effects outside its sufficient and autonomous self. During those two millennia theorists and critics did not group into a single class what we now define as "the fine arts," nor did they propose a vocabulary for identifying a mode of response which is uniquely artistic, or for talking about works of art in a way that undertakes to be definitive for them and exclusive of all other human products.

In undertaking to account for this extraordinary change in the way we talk about art, we need to bring into prominence the fact that modern theories of art-as-such have an implicit understructure which is alien to earlier theorists. Modern theories assume a connoisseur's stance toward the finished work of art, and many of them analyze the distinctive features of this stance on the basis of what I shall call "the contemplation model." That is, when we set out to analyze or define the nature of art and of our experience of art, we assume as paradigmatic a situation in which a perceiver confronts an isolated work, and we usually describe his response as an exclusive attention to the features it presents to his absorbed contemplation. T. E. Hulme expressed tersely the connoisseur's point of view and the contemplative model. "Contemplation," he defined as "a detached interest."

> The object of aesthetic contemplation is something framed apart by itself and regarded without memory or expectation, simply as being itself, as end not means, as individual not universal.[1]

In 1960 Jerome Stolnitz introduced his *Aesthetics and Philosophy of Art Criticism* by reference to "the aesthetic attitude," which he defined as a "disinterested and sympathetic attention to and contemplation of any object of awareness whatever, for its own sake alone." Resort to the aesthetic attitude has, since the 1920s, become one of the most common ways to establish the nature of art by primary reference to the experience of the percipient, and in Stolnitz we find its standard consequences. The attitude of aesthetic contemplation can be taken toward "any object of awareness whatever," whether it is a natural object or something made by man. And a work of fine art, no less than a work of nature, is confronted as a completed object, however it got made. The fact that it is a human product, made by human design, becomes a secondary consideration; it is simply regarded as an object especially adapted to aesthetic contemplation, and so constituted as richly to reward such contemplation. But the attributes of the work of art, so established, coincide with the internal self-sufficiency attributed to it by the New Critics and other theorists who base their theory of art-as-such primarily on the nature of the work itself, rather than on the attitude of the percipient. The work, as Stolnitz puts it, is to be regarded "as a self-contained object which is of interest in its own right."

> Whenever we are talking about works of art as aesthetic objects, we should make sure that we are talking about what is in the work itself. If we are not, then what we say is a gross confusion. . . . The work of art, when considered as an aesthetic object, has a significance and value which is inherent in itself alone.[2]

In sharp contrast, theorists from classical Greece until the eighteenth century discussed the arts within a totally different frame of reference; they assumed the maker's stance toward a work, and analyzed its features in terms of a construction model. The term "the arts" itself was used in the classical era to identify the total class of things which are not found in nature, but are brought into being by human contrivance—a class that included shoemaking and farming as well as painting and sculpture; and the term *techne* or *ars* referred to the particular principles and skills, teachable to all those who are born with the requisite talents, which a human being applies to produce a specific kind of product. The Greek *poiema* (Latin, *poema*) signified a "made thing," in accordance with a *poiesis* (*poesis*)—an art or mode of making—put to use by a *poietes* (*poeta*), or maker; and in the European languages, "poet" and "maker" remained interchangeable terms through the Renaissance. Traditional critical theorists, as well as writers of technical manuals, treated their subject in terms of the requisite elements and principles for constructing an artistic product, and they applied their analysis not to "the arts" in general, but to a single art, most often poetry, or to a subclass of poetry such as tragedy, which they paralleled only occasionally, and only in selected aspects, with one or more of what we now call the other "fine arts"; and their critical treatises were designed no less to guide a poet in writing a good poem than to help the critic in judging whether, and in what ways, a poem is good or bad. In this aspect Aristotle's *Poetics*, despite its important differences, is at one with the rhetoricians, with Horace, and with Longinus—those classical theorists who, as they became known, established the basic modes and terms for dealing with a fine art which persisted through the seventeenth and into the eighteenth century.

As James Hutton emphasizes, "It must always be kept in mind that the *Poetics* is not about poetry in some vague sense of the word but about the art of poetry; it is an 'art' or *techne* (how to compose successful poems), but an 'art' that is founded on a scientific understanding of the subject." "Everything is viewed from within the poet's art."[3] Aristotle's opening statement makes clear his constructional approach to the elements and ordering principles of each kind of poem:

The art of poetry, both in its general nature and in its various specific forms, is the subject here proposed for discussion. And with regard to each of the poetic forms, I wish to consider what characteristic effect it has, how its plots should be constructed if the poet's work is to be good, and also the number and nature of the parts of which the form consists.

Classical books on rhetoric were designed to show how one constructs a discourse that will exploit all available means to effect persuasion in an audience on any given subject and occasion. And Horace's *Ars Poetica*, expressly addressed to an aspiring poet, lays out the way to compose poems that will have the greatest possible success with a discriminating reading public. That work will be most widely acclaimed in which the poet includes both the useful and the pleasurable, *utile et dulce*, in order *prodesse et delectare*, both to instruct and to delight the audience; to which later theorists added a third term from Cicero's statement of the functions of rhetoric: not only to teach and to please, but to evoke emotion. In the Middle Ages and the Renaissance, selected topics from classical treatments of the art of poetry—at first (and almost always predominantly) from Horace's *Ars Poetica*, then from Aristotle, and finally from Longinus—got applied to painting and then to others of "the fine arts." It is clear, however, that from the point of view of the construction model, the patent differences in the materials and required skills of a poet effecting a work of verbal art, a painter wielding a brush, a sculptor hewing marble or casting bronze, an architect designing an edifice, and a composer deploying tones to form a melodic and rhythmic product, would keep such diverse arts from being classified together in any systematic fashion; and they in fact remained largely separate in theory until the end of the seventeenth century.[4]

Given the long life of this way of dealing with the separate arts, it is plausible to assume that the grouping of all the fine arts under the defining criteria of art-as-such—that is, as independent and self-sufficient entities—is taken for granted by many of us, in part at least, because it is built into our current language for discussing the arts. I shall sketch the emergence of the concepts of art-as-such—especially in the radical form of the contemplation model—and then go on to identify the intellectual prototypes whose availability and familiarity to philosophers may account not only for the precise features of this unprecedented theory of art, but also for the speed with which, once introduced, the new theory was accepted and exploited.

I.

The theory of art-as-such was not a product of late nineteenth-century aestheticism and its laudation of *l'art pour l'art*. It both originated and came to fruition in the course of the eighteenth century. Crucial was the turn from the traditional perspective on the arts as diverse modes of making to the new perspective on each work of art as a completed object which is attended to by a perceiver. This shift in the controlling paradigm is apparent in all three of the new ways of reasoning about art which appeared in the eighteenth century. It constituted the framework of the Neoplatonic consideration of life and art, according to a play of analogy between the human contemplation of higher and lower modes of being, in the *Characteristics* of the third Earl of Shaftesbury, published 1711. It was manifested that same year, in a very different mode, in the epochal, although seemingly casual, *causeries* by Joseph Addison on "The Pleasures of the Imagination": Addison assumes as paradigmatic the situation in which a spectator confronts an object and proceeds, in the empirical fashion of Locke's philosophy of perception, to analyze the causal relations between features of the object and the pleasurable responses of the percipient mind. A parallel shift of paradigm is evident in the German "rationalists" of the school of Leibniz and Christian Wolff who undertook, in quasi-geometric fashion, to deduce empirical truths from self-evident premises. The founding texts of this third way of treating the arts were the writings of Alexander Baumgarten, his *Philosophical Reflections on Poetry* in 1735 and his *Aesthetica* in 1750. Baumgarten coined the term "aesthetics" and established the area of concern that it designated as a standard branch of philosophy; his definition of aesthetics as "the science of sensuous knowledge," and his definition of a poem as "a perfect sensuous discourse," reveal his adoption of a specific kind of cognition by a perceiving mind as the ground from which, *more geometrico*, he undertakes to deduce the essential features of a work of art. Since all three modes of theorizing take the point of view, not of the artistic craftsman, but of the connoisseur, the differences in skills, media, content, and aims of the hitherto diverse arts drop out of essential theoretical account. Instead, these arts tend to be grouped together (and in Shaftesbury and Addison to be largely equated, as objects of enjoyable regard, with beautiful things in nature), and are assumed to possess common features which qualify them to perform their common social role: their role, in other words, as objects conducive to the connoisseur's pleasurable attention.

In 1790, only eight decades after Shaftesbury had established the Platonic contemplator, and Addison the Lockean spectator, as the generative center of artistic theory, the concepts of art-as-such achieved a full development in Immanuel Kant's *Critique of Aesthetic Judgment*. Philosophic commentators on Kant's theory concern themselves, properly enough, with the matters constituting the bulk of his *Critique*; that is, his analysis of the complex play of the mental faculties in aesthetic experience, and especially his attempt to demonstrate that an individual's "subjective" judgment that an object is beautiful, since it makes a tacit claim for agreement by all mankind, involves an a priori principle which is common to all minds. My concern, however, is not with Kant's elaborate philosophical superstructure, but only with what he takes for granted; and that is, the normative experience of an object of aesthetic attention. And in this respect we find that Kant simply accepts certain aspects, already severally current in English and German thought, as defining aesthetic experience. He does not argue for or against these defining attributes. Instead he systematizes them, and occupies himself with showing how this "unique" mode of experiencing an object aesthetically (which he calls "the judgment of taste") is, as he puts it, "possible"; that is, how it can be accounted for, by reference to distinctive operations of the inherent faculties that the mind brings to all its experience—the same faculties which Kant had posited, in his earlier two *Critiques*, to account for the possibility of valid knowledge and of valid moral decisions.

Nietzsche long ago remarked that "Kant, like all philosophers, instead of viewing the issue from the side of the artist, envisaged art and beauty solely from the 'spectator's' point of view."[5] Nietzsche is right, in that Kant takes as paradigmatic an encounter between a perceiver and an object which is held isolatedly in attention, and is "immediately"—that is, without intervening thought, or reference to a "concept"—experienced pleasurably as being "beautiful," or as possessing "aesthetic quality" [*aesthetische Beschaffenheit*]. But I would specify that Kant's model for analyzing this encounter is not the Addisonian spectator, but a contemplator—a model with a very different philosophical provenience. In Kant's summary statement: a "pure" judgment of taste "combines delight or aversion immediately with the bare *contemplation* [*blossen Betrachtung*] of the object irrespective of its use or of any end."[6] Such a judgment, it should be remarked, is "pure" in that it satisfies all, and only, the necessary and sufficient criteria for being accounted an aesthetic judgment—without, that is, any superfluous or conflicting elements.

The analyzable aspects ("moments") of the aesthetic judgment which Kant details coincide with the concepts and the philosophical vocabulary which I have specified for art-as-such. The crucial aspect is that this judgment is "disinterested," or "independent of all interest"—"taste in the beautiful," Kant further specifies, "is the one and only disinterested [*uninteressiertes*] and *free* delight" (pp. 42, 49). The judgment is disinterested in that it is "purely contemplative [*bloss kontemplativ*]," hence entirely distinct from the "interested" judgments of what is "agreeable" or "useful," or "the moral good" (p. 48). As "mere contemplation," aesthetic perception must also be "indifferent . . . to the real existence of the object," and can have no reference to one's desire to possess the object, or to any function that the object may serve as a means to an "external" end (pp. 43, 48–49). The pure contemplation and judgment of its beauty is independent even of the emotion an object may evoke in the percipient (pp. 65, 68). The contemplated object, Kant says, thus "pleases for its own sake [*für sich selbst gefällt*]" (p. 90). And the beauty of an object, whether in nature or in art, is experienced, in Kant's noted phrase, as *"Zweckmässigkeit ohne Zweck"* [purposefulness without a purpose]—it has no determinate purpose, yet achieves the purpose it doesn't have (pp. 69, 86). That is, the beauty of a thing, whether natural or an artifact, "appears as if it were preordained" precisely to effect the pleasurable aesthetic judgment or response, yet it is not referable to any express purpose, or intention, on the part either of a natural agency or of a human agent to make it serve that end (pp. 91, 61–62, 216). A beautiful work of art, no less than a beautiful object in nature, may thus be said to have no determinate end except to be just what it is for our disinterested aesthetic contemplation.

It is important to note that it is only after Kant has fully established the essential features of general aesthetic experience—effected by a beautiful rose or birdsong no less than by a work of art—that he goes on, in the second book of the *Critique*, to discuss *die schönen Künste*, or fine arts. His list of the major arts is the one that had already become, and still remains, the standard one of poetry, painting, sculpture, architecture, and music; he includes also eloquence and landscape gardening. In this section of his work, Kant deals with the production of a work of art. His aim, however, is not, as in traditional theories based on the construction model, to establish the principles by which an artist selects, modifies, and orders the elements of a work of art in order to effect deliberate artistic ends. Instead, a chief enterprise is to explain how it is possible (in terms of the interplay of the productive faculties of the mind) that an artist, whatever his ruling concepts and ends, manages nonetheless to achieve a work which is adapted to the disinterested, concept-free, and end-independent "pure judgment of taste." Kant's problem, in other words, is to show how it can be that an artist, without intending to do so—and in fact while often intending quite different ends—effects a product which meets the precise criteria which Kant had already established by reference to the contemplation model of the encounter between a percipient and a ready-made aesthetic object.

In line with this philosophical enterprise, for example, Kant distinguishes the degree to which architecture and painting are unqualifiedly a "fine art," or "free art," in the sense of being independent of an "ulterior end." In a work of architecture, the "essential character" is "the adaptation of the product to a determinate use," and the very "form" of a building is not taken from nature, but is determined by this "arbitrary end." Its character as a fine art consists in the way the building presents itself to us in this intentional aspect, "yet at the same time as aesthetically purposive [*äesthetisch-zweckmässig*]"—in other words, so as to manifest that purposiveness-without-purpose which, when it is viewed as an object of aesthetic contemplation, is a necessary condition for our judgment that it is a beautiful building. "On the other hand," Kant says, "a pure [*blosses*] piece of sculpture" is "made solely to be looked at and must please for its own sake [*für sich selbst gefallen soll*]"; although, as a corporeal imitation of something in nature its sensuous truth "must not go so far as to lose the appearance of being an art," hence "a willed product [*Produkt der Willkür*]" (pp. 186–87). So also with paintings "in the true sense of the word"— that is, paintings "which are not intended *to teach* such matters as history or natural science"; these "are there entirely to be looked at [*zum Ansehen*], in order to . . . engage the aesthetic judgment independently of a definite end" (p. 188).

Aspects of Kant's theory were quickly adopted, and adapted to a variety of metaphysical contexts, by a number of German philosophers, from Schiller, Schelling, and Friedrich Schlegel to Hegel and Schopenhauer; so that the assumption that an artifact, insofar as it is a work of fine art, is to be contemplated in and for itself entered the mainstream of aesthetic philosophy. I want to emphasize the suddenness, the rapidity, and the completeness of this Copernican revolution in the theory of art. In the course of a single century, human products ranging from poetry and painting to music and architecture, entirely diverse in their materials, in their required skills, in the expressed aims of their individual makers, and in the occasion and social function of individual works—products which had been classified with other crafts, some of them even with mathematics and the natural sciences, and which had only occasionally and in selected aspects been linked one to another—came to be systematically treated as "the fine arts": a single and entirely distinctive class. The construction model, in terms of which the individual arts had been treated, like carpentry or harness-making, primarily as a procedure for selecting and adapting elements to each other and to preconceived ends and uses, was replaced by the contemplation model, in terms of which all works of fine art were regarded as existing simply to be attended to for the pleasure of doing so. And the essential attribute predicated for the fine arts, distinguishing them from all practical and moral concerns, was that each work is to be contemplated disinterestedly, for its own sake and inherent value, independently of reference to ordinary life or the outer world, or to any relations or ends outside the sufficiency of the work itself.

I don't believe that we can account for so radical and thorough a change by reference to the internal dynamics of the ideas constituting the theory of art. An adequate explanation, for example, must take into account the altering social conditions of the arts in the eighteenth century, and the rapid proliferation of new institutions for making each of these arts available, outside its original social situation, for the appreciation of an ever-growing public; the result was to make connoisseurship—the stance of a spectator, auditor, or reader to a completed and isolated work of art—the normal one for the public, and the normative one for theorists and critics of the arts. That sociological topic, however, must be reserved for another occasion.[7] The question I shall pose now is this one: Whatever the changing historical circumstances which required, or at least fostered, a new kind of art theory, was there at hand an intellectual prototype that would satisfy the requirement, and whose familiarity to philosophers might explain why the theory of art-as-such, once brought into criticism, developed so rapidly and was accepted so readily and so widely?

I think it can be shown that both the point of view and the philosophical idiom constituting the new theory of art were, in a systematic form, commonplaces—very familiar commonplaces—which long predated the eighteenth century; that they had their place, however, not within traditional discussions of the arts, but within the realm of metaphysics, and especially of theology; and that when these ideas were imported into, and specialized for, the theory of the arts, their novelty was not a novelty of content but merely of application.

II.

We can begin with the emergence of the crucial concepts that a work of art is contemplated, and that this contemplation is disinterested. It was not Addison, the empirical analyst of the pleasurable and nonpossessive responses of a spectator to a beautiful object, but the Earl of Shaftesbury who, in the essays collected in *Characteristics* (1711), introduced and set current the specific terms "contemplation" and "disinterested" in connection with the arts;[8] primarily among thinkers in Germany, where the climate of metaphysical speculation made them much more receptive than the English to Shaftesbury's way of thinking. The first thing to note, however, is that the subject of Shaftesbury's elaborately urbane essays is neither aesthetics nor art, but morals, religion, and the lifestyle appropriate to a gentleman, and that in this inquiry he takes his concepts not from earlier theories of the arts but from a philosophical tradition of the *summum bonum*, the nature of the ultimate human good. Shaftesbury's writings are directed especially against the views of seventeenth-century empiricists, represented at a notorious extreme by Thomas Hobbes, that all human conduct is grounded on "self-interest" or "self-love," as well as against the related views of a utilitarian religion, in which the bases of piety are held to be the desire for reward and the fear of punishment. In his counterclaims Shaftesbury renounces the empirical tradition of his tutor, John Locke, and reverts instead to the opponents both of this tradition and of egoistic morality and religion. Shaftesbury, that is, adopts the dialectical reasoning of the Cambridge Platonists, in which (1) the normative concepts of beauty, goodness, and truth are conflated, and (2) consideration of the modes in which these norms manifest themselves proceeds by a play of analogy between higher and lower realms of being. In Shaftesbury's moral scheme the topic of beauty—including the beauty both of natural objects and of works of art—enters because, as he says, "beauty and good are still the same," and "all beauty is truth," in that all three share the essential formal features of harmony and proportion: "What is beautiful is harmonious and proportionable; what is harmonious and proportionable is true; and what is at once both beautiful and true is, of consequence, agreeable and good."[9] And in the play of Shaftesbury's dialectic, all our sensible experiences of things which are beautiful are referred to their supersensible "original" and criterion, which he calls "beauty itself," the "supreme and sovereign beauty," the "divine beauty," "the principle, source, and fountain of all beauty" (II, 128–33).

In his own life Shaftesbury was, in his own term, a "virtuoso"—that is, a connoisseur—of what were soon to be classified as the fine arts. In his essays he sets forth the stance of the gentleman-virtuoso as exemplary for the stance of the gentleman to instances of virtue and moral goodness. "One who aspires to the character of a man of breeding and politeness is careful to form his judgment of arts and sciences upon right models of perfection," and therefore seeks out "the truest pieces of architecture, the best remains of statues, the best paintings," as well as that music "which is of the best manner and truest harmony." But since beauty and good are, in their essential harmonious principle, the same, and the "right taste" for beauty is equivalent of the right taste for what is good in character and conduct, Shaftesbury is able to assert that "the science of virtuosi and that of virtue itself become, in a manner, one and the same" (II, 217–18).

What, then, is the stance of the connoisseur, or of what Shaftesbury calls "the virtuoso-passion, the love of painting and the designing arts of every kind"? Shaftesbury describes it as a mode of love which manifests itself in an unpossessive, nonutilitarian viewing of the beauty of a work of art for itself— "beauties, where there is no possession, no enjoyment or reward, but barely seeing and admiring" (II, 270, note). The response to such sensible beauties is immediate, unreflective, and coercive: such "shapes, motions, colours, and proportions . . . being presented to our eye, there naturally results a beauty or deformity." In a strictly analogous way "the mind which is spectator or auditor of other minds . . . finds a foul and fair, a harmonious and a dissonant as really and truly here as in . . . representations of sensible things"; at least, he adds, "in all disinterested cases" (I, 251–52). To this set of terms for the way we manifest our love of beauty Shaftesbury adds the portentous word "contemplation." "Every real love," he says, is "the contemplation of beauty either as it really is in itself or as it appears imperfectly in the objects which strike the sense"; an example of the latter type is "the contemplation of the ocean's beauty" (II, 126–27). Thus Shaftesbury introduces into his discussion of the way we regard beauty, whether in its primal form, in nature, in virtue, or in works of art, the concept of a contemplation which is disinterested, hence without reference to possession, to personal desires or concerns, or to utility; and he classifies such contemplation, very strikingly, as a manifestation of "love."

Shaftesbury had at hand an exact prototype of a love which finds its satisfaction in the impersonal and absorbed contemplation of an object of supreme beauty—a prototype which was available to him both in a classical and a Christian formulation. In its classical form this prototype is Plato's representation of the ultimate essence, the criterion-Idea which, in its unison of Beauty, Goodness, and Truth, is the terminus of all human desire. Socrates declares in the *Symposium* that what "love wants and has not" is "beauty," and that "in wanting the beautiful, love wants also the good." He then proceeds to recount, and consent to, Diotima's description of the ascent of the lover from the beauty of physical bodies to the beauty of the mind, then to the "beauty of institutions and laws," to culminate in the contemplation, "with the eye of the mind," of "beauty absolute, separate, simple, and everlasting."

> "This, my dear Socrates," said the stranger of Mantineia, "is that life above all others which man should live, in the contemplation of beauty absolute . . . the true beauty, the divine beauty, I mean pure and clear and unalloyed . . . simple and divine." (*Symposium*, 201, 210–12)

This absolute also constitutes the Idea of the Good in *The Republic*, which is at the same time the ultimate Beauty and Truth, of which the "beatific vision," or "divine contemplation" by "the mind's eye," is the final stage of knowledge and the highest value in life (*Republic*, 507–18).

In *Philebus* Plato makes explicit what is already implied in these passages, that this ultimate Idea of beauty and goodness is perfect in the sense that it possesses *autarkeia*, utter self-sufficiency. The Good, the "contemplation" of which constitutes true wisdom, "differs from all other things" in that it "always everywhere and in all things has the most perfect sufficiency, and is never in need of anything else." This Good involves in itself "Beauty, Symmetry, Truth"; and the claims "both of pleasure and mind to be the absolute good" are invalid "because they are both wanting in self-sufficiency and also in adequacy and perfection" (*Philebus*, 59–60, 65, 67). Self-sufficiency, a total independence of relationship to anything outside oneself, is also the essential attribute of Aristotle's God: "One who is self-sufficient . . . is capable of living alone. This is especially evident in the case of God. Clearly, since he is in need of nothing, God cannot have need of friends, nor will he have any." Aristotle adds that "the choice, then, or possession of the natural goods . . . [which] will most produce the contemplation of God . . . is best."[10] In the *Enneads* of Plotinus, the Absolute is likewise endowed with a self-bounded self-sufficiency which makes the selfless contemplation of its essential beauty and goodness the goal of all love and the ultimate human value. "Seeking nothing, possessing nothing, lacking nothing, the One is perfect," thus "wholly self-sufficing," "self-closed," "supremely adequate, autonomous, all transcending, most utterly without need."[11] Since this essence is the ultimate residence and source of "Beauty, which is also the Good," the highest good of the human soul, impelled by "the passion of love," is to rise from the beauties of sense to the nonsensible vision of the One. Then and only then the soul "contemplates Absolute Beauty in Its essential integrity . . . perfect in its purity." And in passages of great consequence for Christian thought, Plotinus describes this contemplation as an act of "perfect surrender" of the self which is

> the soul's peace, outside of evil . . . here it is immune. . . . He is become the Unity . . . no movement now, no passion, no outlooking desire . . . reasoning is in abeyance and all Intellection and even . . . the very self. . . . He has in perfect stillness attained isolation . . . utterly resting he has become very rest.[12]

By various fathers of the Eastern Church, including Origen, Athanasius, and Gregory of Nyssa, the self-sufficient Absolute of Plato and Plotinus was merged with a very different Being— the personal God of the Old and New Testament.[13] Pseudo-Dionysius, the Christian Platonist of the fifth century, made widely current this conflation of a metaphysical principle with the Deity of revelation; and by the sixth century the concept of God as absolute beauty as well as absolute goodness, whose perfection entails self-sufficiency, and who is to be contemplated as the terminus of human love and desire, "had captured," as Wladyslaw Tatarkiewicz says, "the Christian world and influenced all forms of Christian thinking."[14]

But as William James remarked, "I can hardly conceive of

anything more different from the absolute than the God, say, of David or Isaiah."[15] There are very few passages in Scripture which can be construed, even by a freewheeling exegesis, to predicate beauty as a divine attribute, much less to assert that God is ultimate beauty; and the Platonic concept of an Absolute to be contemplated in the perfection of its self-enclosed sufficiency is patently alien to God, the creator, who walked in the garden of Eden in the cool of the day, or to the God who assumed a lowly human form and was crucified with thieves, or to the just but angry God of the *dies irae*.[16] It was St. Augustine who, a generation earlier than the Pseudo-Dionysius, introduced into Western theology the pagan doctrine that the highest human good is a contemplation of beauty absolute, in the course of expounding the most influential and enduring treatment of Christian love outside of St. Paul himself.

Augustine put forward his doctrine of *caritas*, and of its relation to earthly beauties and the ultimate beauty of God, in the *Confessions, The City of God, On Christian Doctrine, On the Trinity,* and various other writings. In his mature thought, the controlling distinction is between *uti* and *frui*, "to use" and "to enjoy"; these serve as criteria for dividing love into two categories: (1) to love something for its use to an end beyond itself, for the sake of something else, and (2) to love something in an enjoyment [*fruitio*] of it as its own end, and for its own sake. All the good and beautiful things of this world of sense, whether these are objects in nature or works of human art, are to be loved only for their use, as a means whereby to ascend to that ultimate goodness and beauty which is God.

> How innumerable are the things made by every kind of art and workmanship in clothes, shoes, vessels and such like, in pictures also and every kind of statue . . . that men have added for the delight of their eyes. . . . But all that loveliness which

passes through men's minds into their skilful hands comes from that supreme loveliness which is above our souls. From the Supreme Beauty those who make and seek after exterior beauty derive the measure by which they judge of it, but not the measure by which it should be used.[17]

Of all beings only God, since he possesses his *bonum* in himself, is self-sufficient, in need of nothing outside himself. And of all things, God and only God is to be loved with pure enjoyment, as his own end and *non propter aliud*, for his own sake (*propter se ipsam*), because of his very excellence, and as Augustine repeatedly says, *gratis*—that is gratuitously, freely, because for no profit outside of him (*extra illum*). The love of God without regard to reward is opposed to self-love (*amor sui*). And the *summum bonum* is to ascend from a love for the things of this world to that *fruitio Dei* which is a *visio Dei*, a contemplation of God in his supreme beauty and excellence. In this life, however, such a vision is restricted to the eye of the mind. Only when delivered from this world into the Kingdom of God shall we achieve that "enjoyment of contemplation [*fructum contemplationis*]" which "will be our reward itself . . . when we enjoy His goodness and beauty"—no longer, as Augustine echoes Paul, "through a glass darkly," but "face to face."[18]

The culminating stage of Augustine's doctrine of love—the absorbed contemplation and enjoyment of God, the ultimate beauty and goodness, for his own sake, as his own end, without reference to personal advantage or to utility or to anything outside his self-sufficient excellence—coincides with the contemplation model, the philosophical idiom, and the defining categories of the doctrine of art-as-such. The change—it is of course a not inconsiderable change—is that God as the sole object of disinterested enjoyment has been replaced by works of human art, and that the eye of the mind, as the organ of such contemplation, has been replaced by the physical eye and ear. It is worth noting, however, that Shaftesbury, like Kant and many later theorists, emphasizes that what the percipient responds to in contemplating a work of art is not its physical or sensuous features but an elusive attribute which they call its "form."[19]

To return briefly to Shaftesbury: That philosopher showed his familiarity with the Christian *caritas* doctrine in his first published work, an edition (1698) of the selected sermons of the seventeenth-century theologian Benjamin Whichcote. In these sermons a principal theme was the moral need to act, not from "self-love" or the desire for personal gain and a "slavish" fear of God, but from "love to righteousness" not as "a *Mean*, but [as] and *End*"; together with the concept that the true love of God is not for "what he is to us" but "for what he is in himself"—that is, for "his own Loveliness, Excellency, and Beauty." Only a mind "Quiet and Serene," Whichcote said, "can contemplate God, and enjoy Him." "The Contemplation and Thought of his Excellency, Goodness, and Perfection, should so fill our souls that Foreign Things should be driven away, and be as it were nothing."[20] In his own "Preface" to these *Sermons*, Shaftesbury attacked the "Ethicks" and the "Political Christianity" of Hobbes. It is a matter difficult to account for, Shaftesbury remarks ironically, that "Men who profer a Religion where *Love* is chiefly enjoyned," of which the exemplar is "the Supream Power" himself, should refer human actions "all to Reward," and so invite for Christian morality the "imputation of being Mercenary, and of acting in a slavish Spirit."

In his *Characteristics*, Shaftesbury makes it entirely clear that his prototype for the concept of disinterested contemplation is Christian as well as Platonic, and also that in describing a love which terminates in such contemplation he is merely echoing a commonplace of "the Christian religion" and what he calls "its greatest principle, that of love" (II, 59). "True piety," he says, is "to love God for his own sake," not "as the cause of private good" or as an "instrument or means of pleasure." He adds that this conception of God as the object "worthy of love and admiration for its own sake . . . is universally acknowledged"—"or at least" as, with his usual social snobbery, he qualifies this claim, "by the generality of civilised or refined worshippers" (I, 269). This love manifests itself in a delightful "contemplation" of the "impowering Deity" as "the source and principle of all beauty and perfection. . . . The peculiar dignity of my nature is to know and contemplate thee" (II, 98). And it is in discussing Christian *caritas* that Shaftesbury brings in the key term "disinterested." The "principle of love" in Christianity aims "at what is called disinterestedness, or teaching the love of God or virtue for God or virtue's sake" (II, 54–55). Such "disinterested love of God" he describes as "a love which is simple, pure, and unmixed, which has no other object than merely the excellency of that being itself, nor admits of any other thought of happiness than in its single fruition"—a term which, in Augustine's Latin, had been *fruitio.*

In Shaftesbury's dialectic by analogy, the loving and disinterested contemplation of the perfect beauty and goodness of God becomes what he calls "the pattern and examplar" both of the way we regard human virtue—the "contemplation . . . of a beautiful, proportioned, and becoming action" (II, 176; I, 296–97)—and of the way we regard beautiful objects in this world—"the contemplation of beauty as it appears imperfectly in the objects which strike the sense" (II, 126–27). But since the play of this analogy is within a hierarchy of levels, Shaftesbury's dialectic entails the conclusion that the contemplation of sensible beauty is greatly inferior to the contemplation of the criterion-beauty of which it is "only the faint shadow." For "how can the rational mind rest here, or be satisfied with the absurd enjoyment which reaches the senses alone?" (II, 126) Hence if in "pursuing beauty" we stop at "the virtuoso passion" which is the love of the "designing arts," we sacrifice "all intrinsic and real beauty and worth for the sake of things which carry scarce a shadow of the kind" (II, 270–71, note).

III.

Shaftesbury's *Characteristics* was the chief bridge by which the theological term "contemplation," together with the ethical-religious term "disinterested," crossed over into philosophical analysis of the way we apprehend beautiful objects, including works of fine art. (The English phrase "the fine arts" obscures the fact, evident in other languages, that in the four or five decades after the *Characteristics*, *les beaux arts*, *die schönen Künste*, *le belle arti*, came to be grouped together, in opposition to "the useful arts," by predicating beauty as their defining feature, or their internal end.) Shaftesbury achieved this historical function, however, because he dealt with sensible beauties only as ancillary to his ethical and religious philosophy, and indeed by virtue of the fact that his dialectic permitted no essential distinction, yet enforced a distinction of levels, between religious, moral, and aesthetic contemplation. In Shaftesbury, therefore, the contemplation of sensible beauty remains related to morality, and is relegated to a distant reflex of the selfless contemplation of the divine, or "original," goodness and beauty.

It remained for Shaftesbury's successors, especially in Germany, where as Herder said he had "signally influenced the best heads,"[21] to complete the process which he had unwittingly begun. They secularized and specialized the terms "contemplation," "disinterested," and "beauty" as well, not only by abstracting them from their earlier theological contexts, but by using them specifically to differentiate aesthetic experience from religious and moral, as well as practical, experience. As applied to the fine arts, the tendency of this process was to detach a work of art from all reference to an external reality or end, and from any relation to anything outside its sufficient self. In most of these philosophers, there nonetheless remain evidences that their views of art are derivative both from the *eros* doctrine of Plato and the Platonists and from the *caritas* doctrine of Augustine and other Christian theologians. Even in our own time, the ghost of its ancestral prototype in the philosophy and theology of love continues to haunt the discussion of the arts, in terms such as "an art lover," or "an amateur of art."

To illustrate the result of this evolution I shall cite Karl Philipp Moritz, a remarkable thinker who, at the age of twenty-nine, published a six-page essay which is the first complete and unqualified statement of art-as-such. This "Essay on the Unification of All the Fine Arts and Sciences of the Arts under the Concept of the Complete-in-Itself [*des in sich selbst vollendeten*]" appeared in 1785, five years earlier than Kant's *Critique of Aesthetic Judgment*. It is directed expressly against the two reigning principles of the construction theory of art—that the "chief aim" of the fine arts is an "*imitation* of nature," and that the purpose of the imitation is to give pleasure to an audience. Only the mechanical or useful arts, Moritz insists, have an "*outer* end," or an end "outside themselves in something other." In opposition to such views he poses a contemplation model for the fine arts:

> In the contemplation [*Betrachtung*] of the beautiful object, however, I roll its end back from me into the object itself; I contemplate it as something which is *completed*, not in me, but *in its own self*, which therefore constitutes a whole in itself, and affords me pleasure *for its own sake* [*um sein selbst willen*].[22]

Moritz dedicated his essay to Moses Mendelssohn, who had proposed that the fine arts achieve their pleasurable aim by the "sensuous expression of perfection [*Vollkommenheit*]," in which the artist exceeds the nature he represents by making "beauty his final and unique goal."[23] As Martha Woodmansee has shown, Moritz severs this view of art from its remaining references to the nature which art represents and to the pleasures at which it aims, by detailed recourse to a specific theological prototype.[24] He had been brought up within a strict Quietist sect, in accordance with the doctrines of Madame de Guyon, which proposed as the highest mode of Christian life a still contemplation in a selfless love of God. Woodmansee cites a passage in which Moritz himself summarized the Quietist creed in his autobiographical novel *Anton Reiser* (1785–90): it stresses "the total annihilation of all so-called selfhood or self-love, and a totally disinterested [*uninteressierte*] love of God, in which not one little spark of self-love must intrude, if it is to be pure."[25]

In treating the fine arts, Moritz salvaged features of his rejected religious creed of a pure and disinterested love—much as James Joyce later salvaged elements of the Catholic creed of his youth—by translating them into the categories of a secular theory of art. The process is patent in this passage, in which Moritz describes "the sweet astonishment, *the pleasant forgetfulness of ourselves*, in the contemplation of a beautiful work of art."

While the beautiful draws our attention exclusively to itself, it draws us for a time away from ourselves, so that we seem to lose ourselves in the beautiful object; and precisely this loss, this forgetfulness of self, is the highest degree of pure and disinterested [*uneigennützigen*] pleasure which beauty grants us. In that moment we sacrifice our individual confined being to a kind of higher being. Pleasure in the beautiful must therefore ever approximate to disinterested *love*, if it is to be genuine. . . . Beauty in a work of art is not pure and unmixed for me until . . . I contemplate it as something which has been brought forth entirely for its own sake, in order that it should be something complete in itself.

Moritz adds that in a work of art an "outer use or end" is replaced by "its inner purposefulness [*innere Zweckmässigkeit*]"; any pleasure that the work may afford its spectator is "fortuitous" or only "by the way." And in a final step, he attributes to the artist the specific intention of producing a self-enclosed object for disinterested contemplation. "The true artist will seek to bring into his work the highest inner purposefulness or perfection [*Vollkommenheit*]; and if it then finds approval [by its audience] he will be happy; but he has already achieved his real end with the completion of the work."[26]

Three years later, after his association with Goethe in Rome, and still two years before Kant's third *Critique*, Moritz published his essay "On the Formative Imitation of the Beautiful." This is a longer and more complex presentation of his views, focusing now on "the question . . . how a thing must be made, in order not to *need* to be useful"; but he repeats his earlier theory that a work of art is made to be contemplated disinterestedly, for its own sake, as an object whose end and value is internal to its own coherent being. To this deployment of what became the standard vocabulary of art-as-such Moritz now adds, and stresses, the criterion of self-sufficiency: A work of art "must *strike our senses*, or be *graspable by our imagination*, as a self-sufficient whole [*ein für sich bestehendes Ganze*]." Moritz thus transfers to the sensible beauty and perfection of a work of human art the Platonic and Christian concept of the self-sufficiency, or *autarkeia*, which had hitherto been an attribute of the divine perfection, and of that alone. Only rapt attention to such a work of art, Moritz adds, can give us peace. "The beautiful object is contemplated and felt, just as it is produced, entirely for its own sake. . . . We contemplate it because it simply is there . . . in those moments in which our restless activity makes place for a still contemplation [*Beschauung*]." Thus the beauty of a sensible work of art, "in which destruction itself is resolved" in calm, "seems . . . to *imitate* that eternal Beauty which is exalted over destruction and formation itself." Moritz ends his second essay: "And from mortal lips no sublimer word can be uttered about the beautiful object than: *It is!*"[27] We can put it another way: What God was, the beautiful work of art is.

It is by now evident that Kant's model of the essential aesthetic experience—of a "pure judgment of taste," whether in response to a beautiful object in nature or to a work of beautiful art—is in the direct lineage of traditional definitions of the *summum bonum* as a "pure" love which culminates in the disinterested contemplation of absolute beauty for its own sake, without reference to personal profit or to external relations or ends. In his own statements of aesthetic contemplation, Kant gives no indication that he had in mind its classical and Christian antecedents. We can be certain, however, that he had thorough knowledge of these prototypes, and in their theological as well as Platonic formulations. He had been brought up in a household strictly committed to the evangelical mode of Lutheranism known as Pietism, had attended a gymnasium devoted to Pietist indoctrination, and had studied theology at Königsberg with the intention of becoming a minister.[28] Kant in his maturity was not a creedal Christian. Nonetheless, he regarded Christian revelation as an imaginative vehicle of truths which can be appropriated and rendered into conceptual terms by philosophic rationality. It is notable that in the decade between the mid-1780s and -1790s, just before and after the *Critique of Aesthetic Judgment*, Kant wrote a series of essays on human history, past, present, and future, which explicitly set out to translate the truths embodied in biblical myths and prophecy into conceptual and empirical accounts of the origin of evil, as well as of the ultimate triumph over evil which we may anticipate in a perfected community of mankind—as Kant put it, "one sees that philosophy too can have its chiliasm."[29] And this much at least is clear: Kant did not invent the conception of the disinterested contemplation of a beautiful object for its own sake, but found its features and vocabulary in earlier theorists, from Shaftesbury through Moritz, in whose writings its provenance in doctrines of Christian love is unmistakable.

It is revealing, in this context, to glance at Wilhelm Heinrich Wackenroder's *Confessions from the Heart of an Art-Loving Friar*, written seven years after Kant's *Critique*. Wackenroder had attended Moritz's lectures on aesthetic theory and criticism, which were a notable event in the cultural life of Berlin in 1789–90, and was influenced by his writings.[30] A passage in Wackenroder demonstrates the tendency of the contemplation model, once it has been applied to works of secular art, to draw with it supplementary aspects of religious devotion—and in this instance, the effusive sentiments of German Pietism. "Art galleries," Wackenroder laments, "are regarded as annual fairs, where we evaluate, praise, and scorn new wares in passing." On the contrary,

> they ought to be temples where, in still and silent humility and in heart-lifting solitude, we may admire great artists as the highest among mortals . . . with long, steadfast contemplation [*Betrachtung*] of their works. . . .
>
> I compare the enjoyment of nobler works of art to *prayer*. . . . We would, in my opinion, have to deal in this way with the masterpieces of art in order to employ them properly for the salvation of our soul. . . .
>
> Works of art, in their way, no more fit into the common flow of life than does the thought of God; they transcend the ordinary and the commonplace, and we must elevate ourselves to them wholeheartedly in order to make them . . . in our eyes what, in their exalted being, they are. . . . That day is for me a sacred holiday which, with seriousness and a prepared spirit, I devote to the contemplation of noble works of art. . . . So long as I shall walk the earth, I shall bear them in my imagination . . . for the consolation and revival of my soul.[31]

IV.

One of the most important vehicles for the transmission of the contemplation theory of art was the treatment of aesthetics in Schopenhauer's *The World as Will and Idea* (1819), in which Schopenhauer reverts from the formulation of Kant to its antecedents in Platonic metaphysics. The artistic genius possesses a capacity for "pure contemplation [*Kontemplation*]" which "plucks the object of its contemplation from the world's course" of phenomenal time, space, and causal and other relations, and so yields a "knowledge of the object not as individual thing, but as Platonic *idea*." By embodying this idea in a sensuous material, the artist provides the percipient of a work of art with a "pure knowing" of the idea which manifests itself as an "aesthetic pleasure" in its beauty, free from all personal concerns, all considerations of utility, and all external relations. It is patent that Schopenhauer's prototype is not only Plato's Idea of "beauty absolute, separate, simple, and everlasting," but even more specifically Plotinus' description—already echoed by Moritz, by way of its derivatives in Quietist theology—of the contemplation of Absolute Beauty as an act of "perfect surrender" which alone provides the soul a "peace" without movement, passion, or desire, in a "perfect stillness . . . utterly resting." In Schopenhauer's rendering, contemplation of the idea as embodied in a work of art allows us momentarily to break free from the remorseless compulsion of the will so as to become a "pure, will-less, timeless subject of knowing that is independent of all relations." In such contemplation, as nowhere in our driven life of practical acting and knowing, we achieve "fulfillment," "peace and calm," "the blessedness of will-less perception." "The wheel of Ixion stands still."[32]

Later in the nineteenth century the application to art of the Platonic—and often the specifically Christian—model of the contemplation of an ultimate and self-sufficient beauty was exploited by artists and critics of art to justify their enterprise against the indifference or open hostility of a bourgeois public whose concern was for the conventional, the moral, and the useful. In America of the mid-nineteenth century, for example, Edgar Allan Poe, contemptuous of his middle-class audience, attacked what he called the "heresy of *The Didactic*"; that is, the demand that a poem, or any work of art, be useful, moral, or true, rather than simply beautiful. There cannot, he asserts,

> exist any work more thoroughly dignified—more supremely noble than this very poem—this poem *per se*—this poem which is a poem and nothing more—this poem written solely for the poem's sake.

For "*that* pleasure which is at once the most pure, the most elevating, and the most intense, is derived, I maintain, from the contemplation of the Beautiful." But Poe reveals that the contemplation of a beautiful poem for its own sake is merely an earthly surrogate for the contemplation of its heavenly archetype:

> It is no mere appreciation of the Beauty before us—but a wild effort to reach the Beauty above. Inspired by an ecstatic prescience of the glories beyond the grave, we struggle . . . to attain a portion of that Loveliness whose very elements, perhaps, appertain to eternity alone. . . . We weep . . . at our inability to grasp *now*, wholly, here on earth . . . those divine and rapturous joys, of which *through* the poem, or *through* the music, we attain to but brief and indeterminate glimpses.[33]

The amorphous French movement whose catchword was "art for art's sake" derived, through Baudelaire as intermediary, from these doctrines of Poe, but to a greater extent from the dominant French philosopher of the era, Victor Cousin. Cousin's lectures on *The True, the Beautiful, and the Good,* delivered in 1817–18, were published twenty years later by his former students, working from Cousin's notebooks under the master's supervision, and went through more than a score of editions.[34] Cousin acknowledged that he had "borrowed" a great deal from the analytic sections of those "monuments of philosophical genius," Kant's three *Critiques*;[35] although he conducted a running battle against Kant's "skepticism," and especially his refusal to base his critical and aesthetic philosophy on God as the first principle. "The ideal," Cousin said, "is the object of the artist's passionate contemplation." "The arts are called *les beaux arts* because their sole end is to produce the disinterested [*désintéressée*] emotion of beauty, without regard to utility, either in the spectator or in the artist." A beautiful object, whether in nature or art, evokes "a sentiment of love for the object which has evoked it," but a love "free from all desire," for "the sentiment of beauty is to itself its own satisfaction." And throughout the lectures, it is clear that for Cousin the conceptual model for the disinterested contemplation of the work of art is the Christian doctrine of selfless love, for the sake of his beauty and perfection, of a self-sufficient God:

> God is beauty *par excellence*. . . . He offers to the reason the highest idea . . . to the imagination the most ravishing contemplation, to the heart a supreme object of love. . . .
> This all-powerful being has indeed chosen to create us without having any need of us. . . . We love a beautiful or a good object because it is such, without prior consideration whether this love may be useful to its object or to ourselves. All the stronger reason that, when it ascends to God, love is a pure homage rendered to his perfections; it is the natural overflow of the soul towards a being who is infinitely lovable.[36]

A consequence drawn from this theological prototype is Cousin's claim that the artistic achievements of fifteenth-century Italy manifest "the faith of art in its own self, and the cult of beauty," and that in all ages "art is also in itself a kind of religion."[37] In his lecture series of 1818, Cousin translated Kant's distinction between knowledge, morality, and the judgment of beauty into an explicit statement of *l'art pour l'art*:

> The pure and disinterested sentiment of the beautiful . . . [is] an internal sentiment, distinct, special, which refers only to itself. . . . Art is not an instrument, it is in itself its own end . . . hence on the same level as morality and religion.
>
> What is required is religion for religion's sake, morality for morality's sake, just as art for art's sake.[38]

Théophile Gautier, the flamboyant representative and propagandist of art for art's sake, wrote in 1847 that "the mere imitation of nature . . . cannot be the end of the artist." The "highest and most philosophical way to view art" is that of *l'art pour l'art*, which signifies "a work disengaged from all preoccupation except that of beauty in itself."

> The program of the modern school . . . is to seek beauty for its own sake [*pour elle-même*] with complete impartiality, perfect disinterestedness [*désintéressement*]. . . . *L'art pour l'art* means not form for form's sake but rather form for beauty's sake, abstracted from . . . all direct utility.

The artist may reflect his personal situation and that of his era, but only "under the condition that the sacred art will be always for him the end and not the means." Undertaking the question, What is the nature of beauty which is the end of art? Gautier cites a number of philosophers from Plato through Kant, Wackenroder, and Victor Cousin, then concludes: "Beauty in its absolute essence is God. . . . It is invariable, because it is absolute."[39]

The Symbolist generation of Baudelaire, Flaubert, Mallarmé developed from such suggestions—which reimposed on Kant's aesthetics the theological context of its origins—a full-formed religion of art, or in Flaubert's term, "a religion of beauty"; as their English exponent, Arthur Symons, noted in 1899, the new literature "becomes itself a kind of religion, with all the duties and responsibilities of the sacred ritual."[40] Art for art's sake, that is, becomes life for art's sake; the artist must lose his life to find his art; and the true art lover is one of those few, out of *"la foule,"* the profane and vulgar masses, who has been elected as initiate and ministrant of the sacred object, the work of art. Central to this aesthetic was "a remarkable will," as Paul Valéry remarked, which had been "predicted and advocated by Edgar Poe," "to isolate Poetry once for all from every other essence than itself" in the "pure state" of "a perfection that is concerned only with itself."[41] In 1862 Baudelaire raised the question "whether the work of art ought to have no other end than *art*, whether art ought to express solely adoration for *itself*."[42] He himself, following the lead of Poe, attacked as "heresies" the requirements of "teaching," "truth," and "morality," on the ground that "poetry . . . has no end other than itself." *"La poésie pure"* is pure in that it is free from external purpose, from reference to an audience, and even from the personal passion of the poet, for "passion is *natural*," and so introduces "a wounding, discordant note into the domain of pure beauty."[43] By Stéphane Mallarmé, Baudelaire's pure poetry is translated into the ideal of the absolute poem. No longer merely a sensuous reflection of the self-sufficing perfection of the metaphysical or Christian Absolute, the poetic work aspires to be itself an absolute, totally disengaged not only from human author and audience, but from any semantic reference to the world we live in; it exists exclusively within the self-enclosed, self-sufficient, self-signifying bounds of its own verbal perfection.[44]

V.

In our own century theories of art-as-such, taking as their paradigm an observer confronting an isolated work of art, fall into two major types. The first of these accords with the spectator model in the empirical lineage of Addison and Burke: the emphasis is on the attitudinal and emotional response of the percipient when his attention is focused exclusively on the artistic object; the idiom is psychological; the analysis often centers on what is distinguished as the "aesthetic attitude" or "aesthetic distance"; and the work of art is regarded as something which is so constituted as to evoke and reward such aesthetic attention. The second type accords with the contemplation model proper, of which the lineage is Platonic and/or Christian: the emphasis is on the nature of a selflessly contemplative state of mind; the idiom is metaphysical, employing terms such as "knowing," "transcendent," "idea," "purity," "ultimate," "essential," and the distinction between "appearance" and "reality"; and the work itself is described as endowed with an integrity and self-sufficiency which require, or promote, the contemplative state. Conspicuous in this latter theory is the tendency of the contemplation model to bring back into discussion of the arts aspects of its Platonic and theological origins which had been deleted in Kant's version, and often, to carry along a variety of associated religious elements as well.

An example is Clive Bell's highly influential theory (1913) that "the essential quality . . . that distinguishes works of art from all other classes of objects" is "significant form," or alternatively "pure form"[45]—an offspring of the view, common in post-Kantian theorists, that the aesthetic response is primarily to the "form" of a work of art, independently of its material medium or representational content. Bell's theory is based on the contemplation model. "The contemplation of pure form leads to a state of extraordinary exaltation and complete detachment from the concerns of life," and "the chief importance of art" is not "in its relation to conduct or its practical utility," but in the value of things viewed "as ends in themselves." To account for such contemplative ecstasy Bell proposes the "metaphysical hypothesis" that when we are moved by "the formal significance of any material thing . . . considered as an end in itself . . . we become aware of its essential reality, of the God in everything . . . the thing in itself, the ultimate reality." Bell also proposes, not as hypothesis but as assertion, that "art is a religion. It is an expression of and a means to states of mind as holy as any that men are capable of experiencing."[46]

More than a century earlier, we recall, Wackenroder had described "art galleries" as "temples" for the solitary contemplation of works of art "outside the ordinary flow of life," had compared their enjoyment to prayer, and had asserted their efficacy "for the salvation of our soul." Thus also, and precisely, Clive Bell: as men and women once went to churches in search of otherworldly ecstasy, now

> they may go to the temples of art to experience, a little out of this world, emotions that are of another . . . as sanctuaries from life—sanctuaries devoted to the cult of aesthetic emotion. . . .
>
> For those who can feel the significance of form, art can never be less than a religion. In art these find what other religious natures found and still find, I doubt not, in impassioned prayer and worship.

Art in fact has the advantage that it is "an undogmatic religion" not tied to a temporal creed, and that it is therefore "universal" and "permanent." As a consequence, Bell says, he is tempted to believe in his "giddier moments" that "art might prove the world's salvation."[47]

In the more recent past the American New Critics were committed to the "autotelic" and sufficient "poem as such" and "literature as such," independently of "external" ends, or of any relation to the author, audience, or extra-poetic world; they zealously defended this aesthetic creed against diverse "heresies" and "fallacies" which violate the integrity of the self-bounded poem; W. K. Wimsatt even brooded at times on the affinities between the autonomous verbal object and the divine *Logos*. Similar indices to the origins of the contemplation model continue to manifest themselves in various philosophers of the fine arts. I shall cite an instance because it is by someone who is both a professional philosopher and a literary artist. In her Romanes lecture of 1976, Iris Murdoch, with a passing reference to Kant, counters Plato's derogation of the arts by transferring to the arts Plato's own doctrine of a love which terminates in the contemplation of absolute beauty. "In the shock of joy in response to good art, an essential ingredient is a sense of the revelation of reality, of the really real. . . ."

> Good art, thought of as symbolic force rather than statement, provides a stirring image of a pure transcendent value, a steady visible enduring higher good, and perhaps provides for many people, in an unreligious age without prayer or sacraments, their clearest *experience* of something grasped as separate and precious and beneficial and held quietly and unpossessively in the attention. Good art which we love can seem holy and attending to it can be like praying. Our relation to such art, though "probably never" entirely pure, is markedly unselfish.

In this felicitous reformulation of the disinterested and intransitive contemplation of a work of art as such, Iris Murdoch has moved from Platonic *eros* doctrine to the Christian doctrine of the love of God. And having paralleled Wackenroder's and Bell's assimilation of aesthetic contemplation to prayer, she goes on to suggest also their analogy between going to a gallery and going to a place of worship: "The calm joy in the picture gallery is quite unlike the pleasurable flutter felt in the sale room."[48]

VI.

The theory of art-as-such is usually proposed as a set of assertions that claim to be timelessly and universally valid. I have tried to show, however, that it is a way of talking about the arts which was developed only some two centuries ago, and that in its recurrent mode as contemplation theory, its central model and defining predicates were imported, ready-made, from doctrines of love in Platonic metaphysics and a Platonized Christianity. To explain the provenience of this theory, however, is not to explain it away. It is only one way of talking about the arts, but the achievement of critics, whether American New Critics, Continental formalists, or structuralists, who have used some version of art-as-such as a working premise shows that it can be a profitable way to deal with the arts, fostering an unprecedented variety of concepts for analyzing the formal aspects and component elements of a work in their complex internal relations. Furthermore, the theory specifies what has now become a very common way in which we experience many works of art, in some circumstances, and it seems relatively adequate for dealing with abstract paintings, or with serialist musical compositions. But when we turn to *King Lear*, or Michelangelo's *Pietà*, or Beethoven's Ninth Symphony, or Picasso's *Guernica*, the concepts of art-as-such are patently inadequate to account for the range of our responses to these works, which implicate our knowledge and convictions about the world, our moral interests, and our deepest human concerns. One can understand the animus motivating Nietzsche's comment that by "the aesthetics of 'disinterested contemplation' . . . the emasculation of art nowadays seeks insidiously enough to create itself a good conscience."[49]

When I first came across this view of art, however, I felt its strong appeal, and I feel it still. The question arises: Why should the claim that a work of art is self-bounded, and to be contemplated independently of all relations to a human author, a human audience, and the world of human life and concerns, serve as the ground for attributing to art its human value—indeed, for elevating it to the highest of all values? The appeal of such a theory, I believe, is not primarily empirical or rational, but the appeal of its profound metaphysical pathos. This pathos inheres in the view, which has endured from Plato through the Christian centuries, that the highest human good is to lose the sense of self and of the world in the absorbed contemplation of a metaphysical absolute or deity whose perfection consists in being totally otherworldly, serenely self-contained and self-sufficient, and for those reasons, to be revered purely for its own sake. Or to carry the analysis a stage farther back, we can say that the appeal of the theory of art as disinterested contemplation is rooted in the same desires and discontents which motivated philosophers and theologians to posit as the *ens perfectissimum*, as the ultimate reality and value, a timeless, immutable, impassive being whose attributes are established by a systematic negation of the temporality, the turmoil, and the passions which are the inescapable conditions of life in this world. The anomaly bears pondering, however, that the temporality, turmoil, and passions of life in this world have always been the subject matter of the literary art with which we are presumed to engage, according to the theory of art-as-such, in an uninvolved, dispassionate, and disinterested act of pure contemplation.

NOTES

1. T. E. Hulme, *Speculations: Essays on Humanism and the Philosophy of Art*, edited by Herbert Read (London, 1936), p. 136.

2. Jerome Stolnitz, *Aesthetics and Philosophy of Art Criticism* (Cambridge, Mass., 1969), pp. 34–35, 209, 211.

3. Introduction to Aristotle, *Poetics*, translated and edited by James Hutton (New York, 1982).

4. On the late appearance in artistic theory of "the fine arts" as a distinctive class of products, see Paul Oskar Kristeller, "The Modern System of the Arts: A Study in the History of Aesthetics," Parts I and II, *Journal of the History of Ideas* 12 (1951): 496–527; 13 (1952): 17–46. So late as 1772 the young Goethe was contemptuous of J. G. Sulzer's systematic attempt to put all the arts into a single class. "What," Goethe asks, "cannot be bound together by such philosophy? Painting and the dance, eloquence and architecture, poetry and sculpture, all out of a single hole." He remarks acutely that the grouping of products so diverse is based on the point of view of the connoisseur: it derives from "certain pursuits and pleasures of men," and serves the aims of "fashionable dilettantes" of art. "But if a speculative treatment of the arts is to be of use, it must be directly related to the artist. . . . For the concern should be solely with the artist. . . . What does the gaping public matter . . . ?" Review of J. G. Sulzer, *Die schönen Künste in ihrem Ursprung*, in *Goethes Werke* (Weimer) 37 (1896): 206–14.

5. Friedrich Nietzsche, *The Genealogy of Morals* (1887), translated by Francis Golffing (New York, 1956), section 3, part 6, p. 238.

6. Kant's *Critique of Aesthetic Judgment*, translated by James Creed Meredith (Oxford, 1911), pp. 29, 87; the stress on "contemplation" is Kant's own. All the following page references are to Meredith's edition. A few of Kant's phrases I have tried to translate more precisely than Meredith.

7. See M. H. Abrams, "Art-as-Such: The Sociology of Modern

Aesthetics," in *Doing Things with Texts: Essays in Criticism and Critical Theory* (New York, 1989).

8. See the important articles of Jerome Stolnitz, "On the Significance of Lord Shaftesbury in Modern Aesthetic Theory," *Philosophical Quarterly* 2 (1961): 97–113; and "On the Origins of 'Aesthetic Disinterestedness,'" *Journal of Aesthetic and Art Criticism* 20 (1961–62): 131–43. See also David A. White, "The Metaphysics of Disinterestedness: Shaftesbury and Kant," *Journal of Aesthetics and Art Criticism* 32 (1973–74): 239–48.

9. Anthony Earl of Shaftesbury, *Characteristics of Men, Manners, Opinions, Times, Etc.*, edited by John M. Robertson, 2 vols. (London, 1900), vol. 1, p. 94; vol. 2, pp. 128, 138, 268–69. Succeeding page references in the text are to this edition.

10. Aristotle, *Eudemean Ethics*, Book VII, "Friendship," sections 1244b, 1249b. It should be remarked that Aristotle's discussion of friendship in this book and in his *Nicomachean Ethics*, as well as Cicero's essay "On Friendship," contributed to later moralists and theologians the distinction between the love for a friend for the ulterior ends of pleasure, utility, and personal gain, and the higher love for a friend for his intrinsic virtue, as its own end. As Cicero put it (*De Amicitia*, pp. xxi, 79–80): "Those are worthy of friendship who have the reason for being loved in themselves [*in ipsis inest causa*]," and the highest friendship "is desirable in and for itself [*per se et propter se*]."

11. Plotinus, *The Enneads*, translated by Stephen MacKenna, revised by B. S. Page (London, 1956), pp. 380, 400–401, 619.

12. Plotinus, pp. 61–63, 409, 622–24.

13. See, e.g., K. Svoboda, *L'Esthétique de St. Augustin et ses sources* (Brno, 1933), pp. 48ff.; Anders Nygren, *Agape and Eros*, translated by Philip S. Watson (London, 1953), pp. 349–446.

14. Wladyslaw Tatarkiewicz, *History of Aesthetics*, translated by R. M. Montgomery, 3 vols. (The Hague and Paris, 1970), vol. 2, p. 31.

15. William James, *A Pluralistic Universe* (New York, 1912), p. 111.

16. On the scriptural texts which served the Church Fathers as grounds for attributing to God the term "beauty," see Tatarkiewicz, *History of Aesthetics*, vol. 2, pp. 4–9, and Edgar de Bruyne, *L'Esthétique du moyen âge* (Louvain, 1947), pp. 7–12. On the merging of the self-sufficient Absolute of Greek thinkers with the biblical God, see A. O. Lovejoy, *The Great Chain of Being* (Cambridge, Mass., 1936), pp. 43–45.

17. *The Confessions of St. Augustine*, Book X, section xxxiv, translated by F. J. Sheed (London and New York, 1944), pp. 196–97.

18. Relevant quotations from Augustine will be found conveniently gathered in the footnotes of Nygren's *Agape and Eros*, especially pp. 503–48. See also Svoboda, *L'Esthétique de St. Augustin*, pp. 102ff.

19. E.g., *Characteristics*, Book II, pp. 131–32: In statues and other "well-fabricated pieces . . . there is no principle of beauty in body. . . . The beautiful, the fair, the comely, were never in the matter, but in the art and design; never in body itself, but in the form or forming power," which is "mind, or the effect of mind." On the elusiveness of Kant's treatment of aesthetic "form," see Francis X. J. Coleman, *The Harmony of Reason: A Study in Kant's Aesthetics* (Pittsburgh, 1974), pp. 112, 156–57.

20. *Select Sermons of Dr. Whichcote* (London, 1698), p. 213; also pp. 147, 151, 216, 409.

21. Cited by John M. Robertson in his "Introduction" to the *Characteristics*.

22. K. P. Moritz, "Versuch einer Vereinigung aller schönen Künste und Wissenschaften unter dem Begriff des in sich selbst Vollendeten," in *Schriften zur Aesthetik und Poetik*, edited by Hans Joachim Schrimpf (Tübingen, 1962), pp. 3–4 (the emphases are Moritz's).

23. Moses Mendelssohn, "Betrachtungen über die Quellen und die Verbindungen der schönen Künste und Wissenschaften" (1757), in *Schriften zur Philosophie und Aesthetik*, edited by Fritz Bamberger (Stuttgart and Bad Cannstatt, 1971), vol. i, pp. 170–73. In his *Morgenstunden* Mendelssohn wrote: "We contemplate [*betrachten*] the beauty of nature and of art without the least motion of desire, with pleasure and satisfaction. . . . It pleases even though we do not possess it, and though we are far removed from the desire to possess it" (*Morgenstunden* [Berlin, 1785], p. 120).

24. "The Origin of the Doctrine of Literary Autonomy," delivered at the Conference of the International Association for Philosophy and Literature, Orono, Maine, May 9, 1980.

25. K. P. Moritz, *Anton Reiser*, in *Deutsche Litteraturdenkmale des 18. und 19. Jahrhunderts*, edited by Bernhard Seuffert (Heilbronn, 1885), vol. 23, pp. 5–7.

26. Moritz, *Schriften zur Aesthetik und Poetik*, pp. 5–8. In his *Götterlehre* (1791), Moritz neatly summarized his view of the nature of the art

object: "A true work of art, a beautiful poem, is something finished and complete in itself, which is there for its own sake, and whose value lies in its own self and in the well-ordered relationship of its parts" (*Schriften zur Aesthetik und Poetik*, p. 196).

27. *Schriften zur Aesthetik und Poetik*, pp. 71–72, 85, 92–93. Friedrich Schlegel, who had assimilated Moritz's "Formative Imitation of the Beautiful," in the mid-1790s supplemented the concepts of internal completeness and self-sufficiency with the term "autonomy":

The unity of the beautiful object as such, as beauty, requires the appearance of self-sufficiency [*Selbstgenügsamkeit*], of internal completeness [*Vollständigkeit*]; and by that very fact makes the merely beautiful object (whose accident and attribute is beauty) into an independent beauty (whose essence and substance is beauty). One could also call this property a maximum of autonomy [*Autonomie*].

"Von der Schönheit in der Dichtkunst," from Friedrich Schlegel's manuscript remains, in *Neue philosophische Schriften*, edited by Josef Körner (Frankfurt, 1935), p. 376.

28. See J. H. W. Stuckenberg, *The Life of Immanuel Kant* (London, 1882), pp. 1–52.

29. See Joseph Pieper, *The End of Time* (London, 1954), pp. 68–105; also M. H. Abrams, *Natural Supernaturalism* (New York, 1971), pp. 204–6, 348.

30. Mark Boulby, *Karl Philipp Moritz* (Toronto, 1979), pp. 207, 222–23. For the echoes of Moritz's theory of art in Wackenroder, see Mary Hurst Schubert, "Introduction," *Wilhelm Heinrich Wackenroder's "Confessions" and "Fantasies"* (University Park, Pa., 1971).

31. Wilhelm Heinrich Wackenroder, *Herzensergiessungen eines kunstliebenden Klosterbruders* (1797), with an introduction by Karl Detlev Jessen (Leipzig, 1904), pp. 100–3. On Wackenroder's Pietist vocabulary, despite his assumed persona of a Catholic friar, see Schubert, "Introduction," *Wackenroder's "Confessions" and "Fantasies."*

32. *The World as Will and Representation*, translated by E. F. J. Payne, 3 vols. (Indian Hills, Colo., 1958), vol. 1, pp. 185–99 (sections 36–38).

33. "The Poetic Principle" (1848–49), in *Edgar Allan Poe, Representative Selections*, edited by Margaret Alterton and Hardin Craig (New York, 1935), pp. 382–85.

34. See John Wilcox, "The Beginnings of l'Art pour l'Art," *Journal of Aesthetics and Art Criticism* 11 (1953): 366–68.

35. Victor Cousin, *Leçons sur le vrai, le beau et le bien*, 23rd ed. (Paris, 1881), p. 140. The first French translation of Kant's *Critique of Judgment* was not published until 1846.

36. Cousin, *Leçons*, pp. 175, 191, 141–42, 169, 424.

37. Cousin, *Leçons*, pp. 185–86.

38. *"Il faut de la religion pour la religion, de la morale pour la morale, comme de l'art pour l'art."* Victor Cousin, *Cours de philosophie . . . pendant l'année 1818, sur le fondement des idées absolues du vrai, du beau et du bien*, edited by Adolphe Garnier (Paris, 1836), pp. 223–24. The first known occurrence of the phrase *"l'art pour l'art"* had also been a rendering, although by hearsay, of Kant's aesthetic views. In his *Journal intime* for February 10, 1804, Benjamin Constant reported a conversation with the youthful Henry Crabb Robinson: "His work on the *Esthetics* of Kant has some very forceful ideas. *L'art pour l'art* without purpose, for all purpose perverts art. But art attains a purpose that it does not have." See Rose Frances Egan, "The Genesis of the Theory of 'Art for Art's Sake' in Germany and in England," *Smith College Studies in Modern Languages*, part II (1921): 10–11; also Wilcox, "The Beginnings of l'Art pour l'Art," pp. 360, 363.

39. Théophile Gautier, "Du Beau dans l'art," *Revue des deux mondes*, 17 (1847), pp. 898–905.

40. Arthur Symons, *The Symbolist Movement in Literature* (New York, 1919), p. 9.

41. Paul Valéry, *The Art of Poetry*, translated by Denise Folliot (New York, 1958), p. 40.

42. Charles Baudelaire, *Œuvres Complètes*, edited by Y.-G. Le Dantec and Claude Pichois, Pléiade edition (Paris, 1961), p. 788.

43. *Œuvres completes de Charles Baudelaire*, edited by F.-F. Gautier and Y.-G. Le Dantec (Paris, 1933), vol. 10, pp. 25, 29–31, 35.

44. See M. H. Abrams, "Coleridge, Baudelaire, and Modernist Poetics," in *New Perspectives in German Literary Criticism*, edited by Richard E. Amacher and Victor Lange (Princeton, 1979), pp. 174–76.

45. Clive Bell, *Art* (1913; reprint, New York, 1958), pp. 17, 54.

46. Bell, *Art*, pp. 28, 54–55, 181.

47. Bell, *Art*, pp. 175, 189, 182–84, 34. Also p. 181: "What might Art do

for Society? Leaven it; perhaps even redeem it; for Society needs redemption."

48. Iris Murdoch, *The Fire and the Sun: Why Plato Banished the Artists*, based upon the 1976 Romanes Lecture (Oxford, 1977), pp. 76–78. Murdoch characterizes Plato's description, in the *Phaedrus* and the *Phaedo*, of our soul's vision, before birth, of the Forms, "entirely separated from the sensible world ('dwelling elsewhere')," as "an aesthetic conception." This passage exemplifies our tendency to read history backwards, interpreting Plato's theory of knowledge according to categories of the aesthetic which were not established until more than two thousand years later—and established on the very model of Plato's doctrine of cognitive contemplation which, by historical reflex, is then regarded as an aesthetic concept.

49. Nietzsche, *Beyond Good and Evil*, section 33.

Spiritual Travelers in the Literature of the West

———

THE JOURNEY OF life is an enduring master trope by which the postclassical West has made sense of human existence by endowing it with purpose, structure, and values. The trope—the Latin term for it is *peregrinatio vitae*—images the life, both of each individual and of the entire human race, as an extended journey through alien lands. Its primary source is the early books of the Hebrew Bible, with their narratives of literal journeys that came to be the archetypes for a variety of figurative applications. The most prominent biblical journeys were the expulsion of Adam and Eve from Eden to sojourn in a fallen world; the punishment meted out to Cain, to wander as a fugitive and a vagabond on the earth; and the exile of Ishmael, son of Hagar, to live as "a wild man" whose hand will be against every man, and every man's hand against him. The most

———

This was the introductory essay to the collection *The Motif of the Journey in Nineteenth-Century Italian Literature*, edited by Bruno Magliocchetti and Anthony Verna (Gainesville, Fla., 1994).

sustained, detailed, and richly suggestive of the biblical journeys is the exodus of the Hebrews "out of the land of Egypt, out of the house of bondage," their long wanderings in the wilderness in quest of the land promised to Abraham, Isaac, and Jacob; the journey of Moses up Mount Sinai to encounter Divinity; and his later ascent of Mount Pisgah for a glimpse of the Promised Land, to which access was denied him but was later granted his people.

The tendency to allegorize these and other stories of expulsions, punishments, escapes, quests, and migrations began in the later books of the Hebrew Bible itself and was given great impetus in the Christian Scriptures. Three scriptural passages—all of them probably written in the middle or later part of the first century—proved to be of great consequence for later forms and applications of the trope of the journey. In his Epistle addressed to the Hebrews (11:8–16), Paul represented the spiritual history of the Hebrew people hitherto in the vehicle of biblical narratives of exile, wandering, and pilgrimage in quest of a promised land—a promise that can now be fulfilled by the higher goal of a heavenly city. "By faith" Abraham and his descendants "sojourned in the land of promise, as in a strange country," but died (as had Moses) "not having received the promises, but having seen them afar off . . . and confessed that they were strangers and pilgrims on the earth. For they that say such things declare plainly that they seek a country. . . . But now they desire a better country, that is, an heavenly: wherefore God . . . prepared for them a city."[1]

The second and closely contemporary passage is Luke 15:11–32, which is explicitly identified as a parable, or short allegory, and is invested with the authority of Jesus himself. The passage represents the spiritual events of sin and repentance in human life in the narrative vehicle of the prodigal son who left home and father "and took his journey into a far country, and there wasted his substance with riotous living." Starving and penitent, he returned to his father, to be greeted with joy and feasting, "for this my son was dead, and is alive again; he was lost, and is found." In the process of time, this parable assimilated other biblical journey-narratives, was endlessly reiterated, and was often used to represent the totality of human history, from the fall and expulsion out of Eden to a coming redemption at the end of time. Of special historical consequence was the fact that the story of the prodigal son figured the spiritual history of humanity as, specifically, a circular journey that ends at the point of departure. Later commentators often interpreted the assertion of Jesus in John 14:6, "I am the way, the truth, and the life: no man cometh unto the Father but by me," as signifying a roundabout journey—from home and father, into a far country, and back home.

The figure of the totality of human history as a circular return was abetted, and importantly supplemented, by a third passage, the vision of the end of earthly history that concludes both the Book of Revelation and the scriptural canon. There the last things—to be accomplished by the God who is himself "the beginning and the end, the first and the last"—are described as a replication of the first things. The creation of heaven and earth "in the beginning" is to be matched by the advent of "a new heaven and new earth" at the end; the original felicity in Eden is to be restored, in that "there shall be no more death, neither sorrow nor crying," for "there shall be no more curse," while the locale of that felicity will include the "river of water of life" and "the tree of life" that had been essential features in the Garden of Eden. What had been a garden, however, is now replaced (as in the Epistle to the Romans) by a city; and this, in a portentous new development, is represented as not only a city but also a woman, "the holy city, new Jerusalem . . . prepared as a bride adorned for her husband." The consummation of history is accordingly imaged as a sacred marriage between the Lamb of God and this woman, his bride, while the compulsion to the human quest for consummation is described—in a way that was to resonate through later Western literature, whether sacred or profane—in the language of ardent desire: "And the Spirit and the bride say, Come. And let him that heareth say, Come. And let him that is athirst come."

Crucial to the development and widespread adoption of the Christian motif of the circular journey were the *Enneads* of the pagan philosopher Plotinus. Writing in the third century, Plotinus formulated a cosmic scheme in which everything emanates from the One (who is ipso facto the Good) through stages of increasing remoteness and division, to the ultimate stage of the material universe and the supervenience of evil. Counter to this eternal procession, however, is a ceaseless "epistrophe," or return to the origin; for "to Real Being we go back . . . to that we return as from that we came." (The Neoplatonist Proclus later formulated this radical metaphysical metaphor as, "In any divine procession the end is assimilated to the beginning, maintaining by its reversion thither a circle without beginning and without end.")[2] Repeatedly, Plotinus represents the longing of the soul to return to its origin in images that are consonant with those in the Christian Scriptures. The soul, for example, is pictured as a lover and the One as the beloved. Alternatively, the soul is described as an errant daughter who abandons her father for a mortal lover but later repents and once more seeks the father, and finds her peace. And in a reading of the Homeric epic that was to be echoed by many later writers, Plotinus interprets the circular voyage of Odysseus as an allegory for each person's internal journey in quest of the spiritual home and father he had earlier abandoned. Plotinus quotes the *Iliad* 2.140, "Let me flee to the beloved Fatherland": "This is the soundest counsel. But what is this flight? . . . For Odysseus is surely a parable to us when he commands the flight from the sorceries of Circe or Calypso. . . . The Fatherland to us is There whence we have come, and There is The Father."[3]

Wherever it came to be known, this world-scheme, with its root metaphor of emanation and return, exerted a profound attraction upon Christian theology, with the result that the personal God of the Bible, creator and redeemer of humankind, was to various degrees assimilated to the utterly abstract and impersonal first principle of Neoplatonic metaphysics. Conversely, however, the cosmic circulation of the Neoplatonic metaphysical system—timeless, unembodied, and as Proclus said, "without beginning and without end"—was by Christian exegetes temporalized, embodied in the process of human history, and figured as a single circle that at its end will return to its beginning, then stop.

By the close of the fifth century all these varieties of the spiritual journey, Christian and pagan, were deployed in the extraordinarily erudite and innovative writings of St. Augustine. He adapted Plotinus' allegoric reading of Homer to the Christian pilgrimage: "Is the sentiment of Plotinus forgotten?—We must fly to our beloved fatherland. There is the Father, there our all. What fleet or flight shall convey us thither?"[4] With this pagan figure of the circular voyage Augustine fused the narratives of exile, wandering, and quest for a promised land in the early books of the Bible, the figurative pilgrimage to "a better country" in the Epistle to the Hebrews, the circular journey of the prodigal son back to the home and father he has left, and the culminating vision in the Book of Revelation of the sacred marriage, supplemented by the candid expressions of erotic desire in the Song of Songs. As a result, Augustine established the full and enduring Christian *topos* of the *peregrinatio vitae*—the figure of fallen man, generic and individual, who wanders as an exile in an alien land, on a toilsome journey in quest of a city in another country that, when reached, turns out to be the home and father he left behind, and that often turns out also to be the dwelling of the bride he abandoned in the beginning. And, on the tacit assumption of early biblical hermeneutics that images signifying the same spiritual thing can be substituted for each other, Augustine often represented the conjoint origin and goal of the spiritual journey as a

conflation of places, persons, genders, functions, and relationships
that bewilders a reader untutored in the interchangeability of the
signifiers in Christian typology:

> Let me enter into my chamber and sing my songs of love to
> Thee, groaning with inexpressible groaning in my pilgrimage,
> and remember Jerusalem with my heart stretching upwards in
> longing for it: Jerusalem my Fatherland, Jerusalem which is my
> mother: and remembering Thee its Ruler, its Light, its Father
> and Tutor and Spouse. . . . So that I shall not turn away but
> shall come to the peace of that Jerusalem, my dear mother. . . .
>
> For that City the friend of the bridegroom sighs . . . for he
> is a member of the Spouse of Christ; and he is jealous for it,
> for he is the friend of the bridegroom.[5]

Through the Middle Ages and beyond, spiritual renderings of
biblical accounts of exiles and journeys, pilgrims and prodigals,
served as commonplaces in numberless commentaries, sermons,
homilies, and works of literature. In extended form, the *peregrinatio* constituted the total plot of that familiar allegoric narrative
in which the protagonist is named Everyman, or Mankind, or
Christian; in which the allegory signifies the normative course of
a Christian life; and in which the goal of the traveler's laborious
and dangerous quest is a land or city where one truly belongs,
which frequently is also the dwelling place of a woman of irresistible sexual attractiveness.

Early in the fourteenth century, Dante wrote the greatest of all
literary instances of this central Christian plot form. *The Divine
Comedy*, Dante's spiritual history, introduces in its opening line
its root metaphor, when the protagonist, "*Nel mezzo del cammin di
nostra vita* [midway in the journey of our life]," is granted the vision
of another journey, with a relay of guides, through hell and up
through purgatory to the verge of the heaven of heavens—thence

to return, though only temporarily, to his journeying in this realm of "the sun and the other stars."

The medieval chivalric romances—with their literal plots of journeying knights, quests, and perilous trials by which the protagonist proves that he merits his lady love—obviously invited adaptation into allegories of the wayfaring Christian life. A late and elaborately designed instance is Spenser's *Faerie Queene.* The plot of the first book consists of the journey, quest, and trials of the faith and morality of the Red Cross Knight and ends with his betrothal to Una in the land of Eden, which he has just delivered from the dragon. This event prefigures the projected ending of the poem as a whole—the successful conclusion of Arthur's protracted search for the Faerie Queene, by whose beauty, seen in a vision, he had been ravished before the beginning of the narrative proper. Almost a century later, John Bunyan wrote the great working-class equivalent of the adventurous quest of the aristocratic knight on horseback, in his story of the pilgrim who shoulders his pack and trudges sturdily through commonplace obstacles, temptations, and perils, toward the celestial city for which he longs. Even in Bunyan's demotic and puritan version, the motivation for the quest continues to be expressed in the language of overwhelming sexual desire. When Christian and Hopeful finally arrive "within sight of the city they were going to," in the land where "the contract between the bride and the bridegroom was renewed," Christian "with desire fell sick," wherefore the travelers "lay by it a while, crying out because of their pangs, If you see my Beloved, tell him I am sick of love."[6]

THE LITERATURE OF the early nineteenth century, especially in Germany and England, was to a remarkable degree a literature of literal, allegorical, and symbolic travelers. One familiar type is the exiled and guilt-ridden wanderer—recognizably on the model of Cain and his later avatar the Wandering Jew—represented by Coleridge's penitent Ancient Mariner and Byron's impenitent Manfred. Another type, like the protagonist in Shelley's *Alastor*, wastes away on a journey in an insatiable quest for an inaccessible object, which is represented as a woman of irresistible allure. Most widespread is the reemployment of the ancient trope of the *peregrinatio vitae*. The representation of the normative life as a toilsome but indefatigable journey toward an ultimate land or place constitutes the plot form not only in the major literary kinds in verse and prose, but also in the many instances of *Universalgeschichte* (a summary of the cognitive and moral history of all humankind, from its origin to its future culmination) and in the genre of the partly fictionalized autobiography. And surprisingly, the same trope is deployed as both theme and organizing principle in the most prominent systems of German philosophy. In its distinctive Romantic version, however, whether in literature, history, or autobiography, the fifteen-hundred-year-old plot of the spiritual *peregrinatio* has undergone a drastic alteration: the goal of the journey has been transferred from heaven to earth and has been internalized and secularized. That is, the journey of life, which had hitherto been a sustained trial for admission to an otherworldly city, is now conceived as a process of self-education, self-discovery, and self-fulfillment in this world. In the economy of statement made possible by German compounds, the Christian *Heilsgeschichte* (salvation history) has modulated into the Romantic *Bildungsgeschichte* (history of education); the goal that justifies the ordeal of human experience is located within experience itself; and that goal consists of the mature identity and assurance of vocation that the ordeal of life's journey has served to form.

A landmark in the transformation of sacred history into a secular process of self-development is Gotthold Lessing's *The Education of the Human Race*, published in 1780. Undertaking expressly to translate the "revealed truths" of the Bible into conceptual terms, the "truths of reason," Lessing converted the scriptural narrative of humankind's fall and coming redemption into the natural history of humankind's gradual education in reason and morality; interpreted the stages of civilization as advancing degrees of the maturation of the human race; and represented the educational process—both of the race and of the individual—in the persistent vehicle of a journey, compelled by an immanent teleology, along a *Weg* (path) or *Bahn* (road) toward a distant goal.

As a thinker of the Enlightenment, Lessing conceived the journey of humankind to be linear, in the mode of a progressive education toward the achievement of rational and moral perfection. The Romantic version of the *peregrinatio*, however, adopts the circular rather than the linear form of the ancient plot, but with a distinctive difference that fuses the concept of progress with that of a return to the origin. That is, the distinctively Romantic educational journey is imaged not simply as a two-dimensional circle but as ascending along a third, or vertical, dimension so as to form a spiral. The educational process, accordingly, is conceived as moving from an initial unity through multiple divisions back to a complex integrity which replicates the simple unity of the origin, but on a higher level. In many versions of the Romantic spiral journey, the place of origin and return is also figured as the home the traveler left behind and toward which he is compelled back by a homesickness for the father, mother, and a lost sheltered place; but this place, once it has been recovered, proves to be of higher status than the original home, because now it has been earned, and as a result is for the first time properly recognized and adequately valued. In many instances the educational traveler is driven also by desire for a female figure, who turns out to be the beloved he heedlessly abandoned at the outset. In this latter mode of the Romantic *peregrinatio*, as in innumerable earlier examples, the father and home to which the prodigal returns has been fused with the bride of the Apocalypse, so that the motivation for the journey is erotic as well as nostalgic. The bride, however, now tends to be conceptualized into an abstract feminine principle, but one that is endowed with infinite allure. In the rendering with which Goethe concludes the second part of *Faust*:

> *Das Ewig-Weibliche*
> *Zieht uns hinan.*

> [The Eternal-Womanly
> Draws us upward.]

This trope of the developing consciousness of the human race and individual as a spiral journey—to reach, at the end, a superior level of its beginning—informs a great variety of literary works in the Romantic era.[7] It is identifiable in Hölderlin's epistolary novel *Hyperion*, as well as in Novalis' visionary prose romance *Heinrich von Ofterdingen*—of which the leitmotif is *"Wo gehen wir denn hin?" "Immer nach Hause"* (Where are we going to then? Ever homeward)—and serves also as a structural element in Novalis' verse *Hymnen an die Nacht*. In William Blake's cosmic myth, the fall of humankind out of a primitive unity and its long recursion to a higher integrity is at times represented as the wanderings of a mental traveler seeking that "sweet golden clime" at the conclusion of his journey; and Blake pictures the consummation of human history as the sexual reconjunction of Albion with Jerusalem, the female contrary from which he was divided at the beginning. In Shelley's *Prometheus Unbound*, after the first act in which Prometheus renounces divisive hate for integrative love, the plot consists of the educational journey of Asia down through the underground realm of Demogorgon up, around, and back to her marital reunion with Prometheus. In his quasi-autobiographical prose fiction *Sartor Resartus*, Carlyle describes how Teufelsdröckh, the foundling who is his protagonist, "lifts his *Pilgerstab* (Pilgrim staff) . . . and begins a perambulation and circumambulation of the terraqueous Globe." The quest of Teufelsdröckh, that is, takes him on a great circle route around the world, during which he ever turns "full of longing . . . to that unknown Father" who might take him to his paternal bosom. This route turns out to be an educational journey through division and anguished isolation to his ultimate recognition that the seemingly alien earth—"now my needy Mother, now my cruel Stepdame"—was in fact the home in which, educated by suffering, he may now return to live as a member of the family of humanity.[8]

German philosophy of the Romantic era incorporated the same radical metaphor as contemporary works of literature—the metaphor of the development of philosophy as a spiraling self-educational journey that ends where it began, but on a higher turning. The major metaphysical systems of that era are never static systems of established truths, but always on the move, compelled by the tension between internal polarities, antitheses, or "contradictions" toward the closure of the circle in an end state that, since all oppositions will be therein maintained but reconciled, constitutes a superior version of the undivided self-unity from which the process originated. And persistently, this progressive systemic movement is rendered in the plot form of a *Bildungsreise* (educational journey), the restless journey of an exiled agent—named "ego," or "subject," or "consciousness," or "Spirit"—in quest of an ultimate reconciliation with its divided other, in a conclusion that is pictured as a return to the place from which it set out, but on a higher level.

Fichte, for example, described *Wissenschaft* (the science of knowledge), as beginning with the unity of the absolute ego, which posits the non-ego and so inaugurates a sustained tension, which drives a process that concludes when it reaches the point at which it "closes with its first principle, returns into itself, and accordingly becomes, by its own agency, completely closed."[9] He also represented universal human history in the pictured form of a circuitous *peregrinatio* of humankind from a paradise of thought-less self-unity toward a recovered paradise, which will be a superior one because it will have been earned by all the endeavors en route:

> The collective journey [*Weg*] which, according to this view, mankind pursues here below, is no other than a way back to that point upon which it stood at the very beginning, and has no other goal but to return to its origin. [Driven out of the paradise of effortless and ignorant innocence, mankind] by effort and knowledge builds his paradise for himself according to the model of the one he has lost.[10]

Friedrich Schelling's *Transcendental Idealism* (1800) presents another version of the division of the unitary subject into polarities that compel a circuitous return to the undivided origin. At one place Schelling describes this process by repeating Plotinus' reading of the Homeric epic as signifying a circular spiritual voyage back to the home that has been left. Alienated nature, Schelling wrote, "is a poem" that, if unriddled, would disclose itself to be "the Odyssey of the spirit which, wonderfully deluded, in seeking itself, flees itself," and will reach its goal only when it "returns completely to itself," as a subject that finally recognizes it is itself the object it seeks.[11]

In his book of letters entitled *On the Aesthetic Education of Man*, Friedrich Schiller repeatedly images the history of civilization as a complex educational journey toward maturity through which "both the individual and the species as a whole must pass . . . if they are to complete the full circle of their destiny [*Kreis ihrer Bestimmung*]." His long essay "On Naïve and Sentimental Poetry" develops this figure, representing the evolution of human culture as a circuitous educational journey in which we (like the prodigal son) arrogantly storm "into an alien land," only to discover that "we desire with painful longing to go back home"—a home that Schiller also identified as "a paradise, a state of innocence, a golden age." But this painful way out turns out to be the way back, although to an infinitely higher form of the innocence and self-unity we have lost. "The road [*Weg*] upon which the modern poets are traveling is the same which mankind must travel, collectively and as individuals. Nature makes him in unity with himself; art divides and cuts him in two; through the ideal he returns to unity." In an important variant of the circuitous journey, however, that Schiller shares with Fichte, Hölderlin, and others, he maintains that, since the goal of the journey is infinite while mankind's powers and possibilities are finite, "the ideal is an infinite which he can never reach," but can only approximate.[12] In this version of the motif we find the common Romantic view that "*der Weg ist das Ziel*," that the goal of the journey is the journey itself, as well as the distinctive Romantic ethos that the proper aim of humankind is an indomitable "*Streben nach dem Unendlichen* [striving after the infinite]," in which the measure of dignity and greatness consists, not in absolute achievement, but in maintaining the discrepancy between an infinite reach and a finite grasp.

Wordsworth described his work as a "poem on my own poetical education," and his account of this education is repeatedly represented as a self-formative journey. The poem opens with a deliberate echo of the exodus from Egypt, as the poet departs on foot from the city that to him had been "a house / Of bondage"; in the course of this walk, which is at first desultory, he becomes "as a Pilgrim resolute" and sets out toward a goal, "the chosen Vale." In Wordsworth's retrospective narrative of his life, many of the crucial episodes are literal journeys on foot, which modulate into spiritual landscapes traversed by a metaphorical wayfarer. Wordsworth deploys the figure of the journey in a double way: On the one hand, he applies the figure to the educational course of his life in the outer world, "from stage to stage / Advancing" until it achieves the "consummation of the Poet's mind." On the other hand, Wordsworth applies the figure internally, to his artistic quest through his memory, in the process of composing the poem that narrates the journey of his life. In symmetry with its first book, the last book of the *Prelude* opens with a literal walk; this time, however, he travels not on a level plain but up Mount Snowden where—in the tradition of definitive visions on a mountain established by Moses on Sinai—Wordsworth recognizes in the cloud-shrouded and moonlit landscape the outer correlation to his own poetic mind and imagination. The close of the poem rounds back to its narrative beginning as Wordsworth, confirmed in his mature identity and vocation as a poet, takes up his "permanent abode" in the Vale that, in the initial passage, he had chosen as the goal of his journey. And in the title of the opening book of *The Recluse*, to which his entire autobiography was designed as prelude, this goal of his life's pilgrimage, in accord with the ancient tradition of the circular journey, is identified as home— *Home at Grasmere*—and is at the same time conflated with Eden. But consonantly with the Romantic pattern of the spiral return, Wordsworth describes his achieved Eden as immensely superior to the original Eden because he has earned it in the painful course of his self-formative journey: "Here must be his Home, this Valley be his World."

> The boon is absolute; surpassing grace
> To me hath been vouchsafed; among the bowers
> Of blissful Eden this was neither given,
> Nor could be given—possession of the good
> Which had been sighed for, ancient thought fulfilled. . . . [13]

Hegel's metaphysical system is in ceaseless motion, and that motion, compelled by an internal, goal-directed tension of successive antitheses, is always circular. "The true," as he describes this timeless circulation in his preface to *The Phenomenology of Spirit*, "is its own becoming, the circle that presupposes its end as its goal and so has it for its beginning." But, he also says, the circling is always a spiraling upward, in that "this return to the beginning is also an advance." The *Phenomenology* narrates the history of the Spirit's painful process toward acquiring the knowledge of systematic metaphysical truth (*Wissenschaft*)—a process that incorporates, within the temporal course of time and history, the timeless spiral pattern manifested in the truth toward which it unknowingly strives. The history of the Spirit, that is, evolves spirally from an original self-unity, through a passing over into its other, then into many successive others, toward the ultimate achievement of a higher reunion with itself. Hegel renders this history in the literary plot form of the self-educative journey of the Spirit, which is represented (in its aspect as the collective human consciousness) as though it were a single protagonist: "The task is to consider the general individual, the self-conscious Spirit, in its education [*Bildung*]," of which "the aim is the Spirit's insight into what it is that constitutes knowledge"—the knowledge that is articulated in Hegel's metaphysical system. Repeatedly this *Bildungsgeschichte*, both of the race and of each individual, is imaged in the traditional mode of the *Bildungsreise*: "To become genuine knowledge," the Spirit "has to work its way through a long journey [*Weg*]"; while "each individual consciousness must also pass through the contents of the educational stages of the general Spirit, but . . . as stages of a way [*Weg*] that has been prepared and leveled for him." This way can be considered as an educational pilgrimage and quest, "the way of the natural consciousness, which presses on to true knowledge."[14]

The denouement of Hegel's protracted quest narrative, which he calls the stage of absolute knowledge, is rendered in the form of a recognition scene, in which the Spirit, now fully "self-conscious," recognizes that the knowledge that has been its goal is in fact self-knowledge. The Spirit, that is, finally becomes aware of its own identity as constituting not less than everything and everyone, all of which had once been alienated from itself, but are now recollected, and so repossessed, by an act of ultimate awareness. This culmination of the self-educative way is a circuitous recursion to "the beginning from which we went out," although now "at a higher level." Hegel images the recursion to the beginning in the time-honored figure of a spiritual return home, although it is a home where the Spirit has all along been without knowing it: at that moment at which the Spirit "has annulled and taken back into itself this alienation and objectification, it is at home with itself [*bei sich ist*] in its otherness as such."[15] And since the homecoming that concludes the educational quest of the Spirit is achieved in Hegel's own consciousness, in his role as both a manifestation and an amanuensis of the Spirit, we in turn now recognize that Hegel's educational history of the Spirit has in fact been—like Wordsworth's *Prelude*—the autobiography of its own protagonist.

The Romantic variation on life as a journey by no means marked the end of the literary uses of the image. So late as the mid twentieth century, T. S. Eliot, in his *Four Quartets* (1935–42), composed the most sustained and intricate deployment of the theme of the journey in all of literature. The whole of Eliot's long poem articulates a figurative quest, by land and sea and underground, for a garden, "our first world," that has been glimpsed and lost but not forgotten. That the journey is circular is indicated by the persistent and paradoxical interplay, in the course of the poem, between the words "beginning" and "end"; and the second quartet, "East Coker," itself enacts that circular shape by opening, "In my beginning is my end," and by closing with the repetition of the opening sentence, with its elements reversed: "In my end is my beginning." We learn that this movement signifies the poet's own educational journey, which (as in Wordsworth's *Prelude*) constitutes a dual education, both in his life and in his poetic craft; and in the traditional way, the place of origin, the unforgotten garden, is identified as home: "Home is where one starts from." This origin turns out also to have been the goal of the quest, for "the way forward is the way back";[16] although, as the end of the *Quartets* reveals, it is not until our circumnavigation has reached its haven that we will achieve the knowledge that it has been, all along, our home:

> We shall not cease from exploration
> And the end of all our exploring
> Will be to arrive where we started
> And know the place for the first time.
> Through the unknown, remembered gate
> When the last of earth left to discover
> Is that which was the beginning.

This is a remarkably inventive poem that, in the way it orders and relates its elements, justifies its reputation as a distinctively modernist work. In those elements themselves, however, we can recognize the Romantic image of the spiral educational journey impelled by a dialectic of contraries; and beyond that, the model of Dante's *Divine Comedy* that Eliot's poem often echoes and emulates; and ultimately, the Augustinian paradigm of the *peregrinatio vitae* as a quest whose goal is not in this world. Eliot's poem epitomizes the long and varied history of the trope of the spiritual journey, even as it attests its continuing viability as an imaginative option.

NOTES

1. Hebrews 11:8–16. All biblical quotations are from *The New English Bible*, edited by Samuel Sandmel (Oxford, 1976).
2. Proclus, *The Elements of Theology*, translated and edited by E. R. Dodds (Oxford, 1933), propositions 33, 146.

3. Plotinus, *The Six Enneads*, translated by Stephen MacKenna and B. S. Page (London, 1956), 1.6.8; see also 6.5.7, 6.5.10, 6.9.9.

4. Augustine, *The City of God*, translated by Marcus Dodds (New York, 1948), 1.9.17.

5. *The Confessions of Saint Augustine*, translated by F. J. Sheed (London, 1944), 12.16, 13.13.

6. John Bunyan, *The Pilgrim's Progress* (London, 1945), pp. 157–58.

7. For a detailed treatment of the motif of the spiral journey in these and other writers of the early nineteenth century, see M. H. Abrams, *Natural Supernaturalism: Tradition and Revolution in Romantic Literature* (New York, 1971), chapters 4 and 5.

8. Thomas Carlyle, *Sartor Resartus*, edited by C. F. Harrold (New York, 1937), pp. 147, 185, 188–89.

9. J. G. Fichte, *Grundriss des Eigenthümlichen der Wissenschaftslehre*, in *Sämtliche Werke*, edited by Fichte (Berlin, 1845), vol. 1, pp. 332–33.

10. J. G. Fichte, *Die Grundzüge des gegenwärtigen zeitalters*, in *Sämtliche Werke*, vol. 7, p. 12.

11. F. W. J. von Schelling, *System des transzendentalen Idealismus*, in *Sämtliche Werke* (Stuttgart, 1856–61), vol. 2, pp. 341, 628. For other references to the *Iliad* and *Odyssey* as a two-part epic of spiritual departure and return, see *Sämtliche Werke*, vol. 6, pp. 42, 57.

12. Friedrich Schiller, *On the Aesthetic Education of Man*, edited and translated by Elizabeth M. Wilkinson and L. A. Willoughby (Oxford, 1967), p. 171; Schiller, "Über naïve und sentimentalische Dichtung," in *Sämtliche Werke*, edited by Otto Güntter and George Witkowski (Leipzig, n.d.), vol. 17, pp. 505–6.

13. William Wordsworth, *Home at Grasmere*, edited by Beth Darlington (Ithaca, N. Y., 1977), ms. D, lines 45, 103–7.

14. G. W. F. Hegel, *Phänomenologie des Geistes*, edited by Johannes Hoffmeister, 6th ed. (Hamburg, 1952), pp. 20, 26–27, 67, 563–64, 549; also, *The Logic of Hegel*, translated by William Wallace, 2d ed. (Oxford, 1892), 379.

15. *The Logic of Hegel*, 379.

16. T. S. Eliot, *Collected Poems 1909–62* (London, 1963), pp. 187–214.

Point-Blank Prose: The Essays of William Hazlitt

WILLIAM HAZLITT AT first planned to follow his father into the Unitarian ministry, became instead a painter of portraits, then turned to writing on philosophy, economics, and politics. Not until his mid-thirties did he discover his vocation as a public lecturer and prolific contributor to periodicals. In the twenty years before his death in 1830, he produced enough to fill almost twenty volumes of his collected *Works*, including superb criticism of English dramatists, poets, and novelists, the best commentaries on painting in the England of his day, remarkable analyses of the English theater and its actors, comments on the contemporary political scene that are of enduring interest, and more than a hundred informal essays which, as David Bromwich says, are "more observing, original, and keen-witted than any others in the language."

Originally published in *The New York Review of Books*, May 10, 1984, under the title "The Keenest Critic." This was an essay-review of David Bromwich, *Hazlitt: The Mind of a Critic* (Oxford, 1983).

In his best-known essay, "My First Acquaintance with Poets," Hazlitt nostalgically recalls the turning point of his life, which was Coleridge's short stay near Hazlitt's village in Shropshire as a visiting preacher to a Unitarian congregation. "I was at that time," Hazlitt says, "dumb, inarticulate, helpless." It was to the example of Coleridge's ceaseless eloquence, in conversation and from the pulpit, that Hazlitt attributes the fact that "my understanding did not remain dumb and brutish," but "at last found a language to express itself." The shy and tongue-tied youth accepted Coleridge's invitation for a three weeks' visit to his home at Nether Stowey in the Lake Country, where he met Wordsworth and heard some of the recently written *Lyrical Ballads* read aloud, at which time, he says, "the sense of a new style and a new spirit in poetry came over me."

But as often occurred in Hazlitt's stormy life, this idyll had a sequel in the form of farce. When five years later he revisited Coleridge and Wordsworth to paint their portraits, his stay created increasing friction and ended abruptly in a scandal. Hazlitt, it seems, was aggressively but awkwardly amatory toward the country girls. As Wordsworth "with great horror" told the story to the painter Benjamin Haydon twenty-one years after the event, when one young woman rebuffed his advances Hazlitt "enraged pushed her down, and because, Sir, she refused to gratify his abominable and devilish propensities, he lifted up her petticoats and *smote* her on the *bottom*." To escape a ducking by the enraged populace, Hazlitt ignominiously fled, assisted by gifts of money and clothes from Wordsworth.

This episode caused an estrangement of both Wordsworth and Coleridge from Hazlitt, which was exacerbated by their increasing political differences and by Hazlitt's outspoken reviews of their opinions and writings. Bromwich treats harshly their rejection of Hazlitt. Undoubtedly, both Wordsworth and Coleridge were intolerant and behaved sanctimoniously toward the younger writer. But in extenuation one should point out that Hazlitt never managed to stay on good terms with anyone for very long. In demeanor he was often gauche, graceless, suspicious—in Coleridge's memorable sketch, he was "brow-hanging, shoe-contemplative, *strange*." He also exhibited what Leigh Hunt called "great impartiality of assault," in that he expressed his mind and variable moods fully, not only about his foes but his friends, and not only in conversation but in print. In the course of his combative life Hazlitt alienated everyone who was most intimate with him, including Leigh Hunt and the tolerant Charles Lamb, who nonetheless continued to praise Hazlitt's qualities when he was at his genial best: "I think W.H. to be, in his natural and healthy state, one of the wisest and finest spirits breathing. . . . I think I shall go to my grave without finding, or expecting to find, such another companion."

In a cogent opening chapter, David Bromwich tells us that his book is about another Hazlitt than the one we commonly admire as a zestful, hearty, worldly essayist; he will reveal a Hazlitt who is "fiercer and less reconciled," the "most restless of the English romantics . . . and in one sense the most shocking." Bromwich claims that as a literary critic Hazlitt is grossly undervalued in our time because of the vogue for theoretical criticism; this, he writes, shows a "love of method and yearning for system" of which "the true father is Coleridge." His complaint is a valid one. To oppose the current academic neglect of Hazlitt as a critic, however, Bromwich takes an unnecessary tack. In his account of Hazlitt's criticism, as he puts it, his own "argument with Coleridge is audible as a persistent undertone." In this argument Bromwich himself succumbs to the modern preference for theory over practice by claiming that, even as a theorist of poetry, Hazlitt is more rewarding than Coleridge; and he employs a seesaw method of evaluation, whereby in elevating Hazlitt he depresses Coleridge and at times comes close to caricaturing his views about poetry.

Both Coleridge and Hazlitt are great critics, but their excellence is different in kind. Coleridge is a systematic critic for whom theory precedes application, and whose theory of poetry is a part of a general philosophy of man and nature. He persistently views the works he criticizes through the perspective provided by his theory, though mediated by his sensibility and subtle awareness of his own procedures as a practicing poet. Historically, Coleridge has proved to be the most seminal and influential writer in our language, both on criticism and on poetry. Hazlitt's special virtues, on the other hand, depend not on a systematic prior theory, but on the immediacy of his response to a specific literary work or passage. If I had to make a choice between them as practical critics, I would, like Bromwich, take Hazlitt's literary commentary over Coleridge's; it is wider-ranging, less moralistic, often more interesting, even startling, in its insights, and more open to the special excellences of such unfashionable poets as Alexander Pope. Fortunately we do not have to make a choice. We can apply to criticism the pluralism that Hazlitt finely asserts for literature: "To know the best in each class infers a higher degree of taste; to reject the class is only a negation of taste; for different classes do not interfere with one another."

Hazlitt decries what he calls the "modern or metaphysical school of criticism," and to identify his own distinctive procedure, introduces the term "impression": "I cannot help receiving certain impressions from things; and I have sufficient courage to declare (somewhat abruptly) what they are." It is difficult to call Hazlitt a critical impressionist without seeming to derogate his achievement, because we tend to apply the term to critics who substitute their own reveries for qualities of the work they ostensibly discuss. Hazlitt means by "impression," however, his direct response to a work's particularities, as adapted, he says, to "the effect which the author has aimed at producing." He praised Edmund Burke in a way that defines his own aim and achievement as a critic. "He loses no particle of the exact, characteristic, extreme impression of the thing he writes about . . . and communicates this to the reader." Hazlitt's firsthand responses to his subjects are of enduring value because they are directed and informed throughout by the play of a well-read, acute, opinionated, and unsystematic but remarkably interesting intelligence and temperament.

The qualities of mind and temperament that distinguish Hazlitt's criticism are revealed in the terms he repeatedly uses to define the highest literary or artistic values: especially "imagination," "genius," "expression," "passion," "character," "gusto," "energy," and above all "power." Hazlitt nowhere pins down the meaning of these words, and all attempts by his commentators to define them are baffled by the variability of Hazlitt's own texts. As Hazlitt used them, they are interrelated and often interchangeable; they refer to qualities of the author's mind, to the work itself, to the objects represented by the work, or to the response to the work by a reader. Sometimes Hazlitt uses them to refer to all these at once. This elusiveness and variability are not defects, but are requisite to the kind of criticism that Hazlitt inaugurated. Because these terms do not designate fixed categories, but are flexible and fluid, they are adaptable to the distinctive quality of whatever Hazlitt is talking about. "A thing," Hazlitt wrote, "is not more perfect by becoming something else, but by *being more itself.*" The meanings of his descriptive words are realized only in the reader's own experience of those features of a work to which Hazlitt has directed his attention.

Hazlitt's most systematic enterprise was his first published work, *On the Principles of Human Action* (1805). A late example of the many replies to Hobbes' view that the sole human motive is egoistic self-interest, Hazlitt's closely reasoned argument, as his subtitle puts it, aims to prove "the Natural Disinterestedness of the Human Mind." Bromwich and other commentators are doubtless right in asserting that Hazlitt later applied the moral concept of disinterestedness to art: it underlies his claim that Shakespeare, "the least of an egotist that it was possible to be," identified himself in imagination with each of his characters. It also underlies his distinction between the outward-looking older poets, from Homer on, and the "modern school of poetry" (by which he meant the contemporary Romantics, especially Wordsworth), who "reduce poetry to a mere effusion of natural sensibility." These claims were widely influential and shaped the opinions of the young Keats. But here Hazlitt was largely refining views current in Germany and England, particularly after Schiller's "On Naïve and Sentimental Poetry," that Shakespeare was both an objective and an imaginatively self-projective poet, and that, like the ancient poets, he was naïve, impersonal, and objective, while the modern poets were predominantly sentimental, self-interested, and subjective.

Much more original in Hazlitt's essays is his emphasis on what he calls "the mixed motives" that compel all human action, including the composition of poetry, and the way that these motives involve "all the intricate folds and delicate involutions of our self-love." The most startling aspect of Hazlitt's criticism is his demolition of the romantic idealism of his contemporaries about the motives for writing poetry, epitomized in Shelley's assertion that "poetry is the record of the best and happiest moments of the happiest and best minds." In "On Poetry in General," Hazlitt asserted that fear, hatred, contempt, no less than hope, love, and wonder, "are all poetry."

> It is as natural to hate as to love, to despise as to admire, to express our hatred or contempt, as our love and admiration. . . . The imagination, by . . . embodying them and turning them to shape, gives an obvious relief to the indistinct and importunate cravings of the will. We do not wish the thing to be so, but we wish it to appear such as it is. For knowledge is

conscious power; and the mind is no longer, in this case, the dupe, though it may be the victim of vice or folly.

As Bromwich says, Hazlitt's criticism is especially interesting for its awareness that "literature and politics belong to one world." He cites Hazlitt's statement "that poetry is an interesting study, for this reason, that it relates to whatever is most interesting in human life," and the most enlightening chapters in his book are those on Hazlitt's political thought and writings, which as he shows belong in the same intellectual and emotional world as his critical thought and his writings on literature.

"I started in life," Hazlitt said, "with the French Revolution, and I have lived, alas! to see the end of it. . . . Since then, I confess, I have no longer felt myself young, for with that my hopes fell." The thinking and imagination of his major literary contemporaries, including Blake, Wordsworth, Coleridge, and Southey, were also shaped by the inordinate hopes they had invested in the Revolution and by their despair at its failure; but what for them was a preoccupation was for Hazlitt an obsession.

> I will never cease, nor be prevented from returning on the wings of imagination to that bright dream of our youth. . . . To those hopes eternal regrets are due; to those who maliciously blasted them, in the fear that they might be accomplished, we feel no less what we owe—hatred and scorn as lasting.

Within this proscenium Hazlitt viewed his own experience, as well as the political events and personages, and the writers and works of literature, of his era.

The persistent term in Hazlitt's writings, which connects, and greatly complicates, his treatment of these matters, is "power." There is in his works, Bromwich notes, "a moral ambiguity implicit in every exertion of power to which the imagination moves us," and the same word links "the power of poetry which Hazlitt loved, and the power of tyranny which he hated." It should also be remarked that the moral ambiguity of power, and Hazlitt's ambivalence toward its manifestation and effects, are evident within, as well as in the interplay between, the realms of poetry, life, and politics. Perhaps the closest we can come to establishing the range of applications in Hazlitt's use of this term is by a negative definition: "power" encompasses essential aspects of human motivation and responsiveness that are left out of account in the moral philosophy of English empiricism, and especially of Benthamite Utilitarianism and its calculus of pleasure.

In the main line of empiricism, which largely governed Hazlitt's early philosophical writings, elementary sense perceptions are accompanied by, or become associated with, pleasures and pains, which give rise, respectively, to desire and aversion, and so to our judgments of good and bad. To this pleasure principle as determining our judgments and actions Hazlitt, in a way that looks forward to Nietzsche and Freud, adds a contrary compulsion, the power principle:

> We are as prone to make a torment of our fears, as to luxuriate in our hopes of good. If it be asked, Why we do so? the best answer will be, Because we cannot help it. The sense of power is as strong a principle in the mind as the love of pleasure.

Hazlitt is writing here about "Poetry in General," but the complex and equivocal role of the sense of power as motivating his own and others' actions and achievements, as well as his responses to the actions and achievements of others, is a dominant theme in his writings about morality and politics as well. He tells us in an essay, "On Depth and Superficiality," that he once startled Coleridge—who as a Christian philosopher affirmed original sin, but interpreted the dogma in a liberal way—by asserting, in answer to Coleridge's challenge whether he "had ever known a child of a naturally wicked disposition," that,

> yes, there was one in the house with me that cried from morning to night, *for spite*. . . . It had a positive pleasure in pain from the sense of power accompanying it. . . . I have no other idea of what is commonly understood by wickedness than that perversion of the will or love of mischief for its own sake. . . . It cried only to vent its passion and alarm the house, and I saw in its frantic screams and gestures that great baby, the world, tumbling about in its swaddling-clothes, and tormenting itself and others for the last six thousand years!

Hazlitt attributed the persistence and success of political oppression not only to the innate delight men feel in wielding power over others, but also to their propensity to identify with the power employed to oppress them. "The love of power in ourselves and the admiration of it in others are both natural to man: the one makes him a tyrant, the other a slave." He rejected the hope that amelioration and reform would someday "complete the triumph of humanity and liberty," because such a Utopian faith requires "several things necessary which are impossible," including the condition that "the love of power and of change shall no longer goad man on. . . . Our strength lies in our weakness; our virtues are built on our vices . . . nor can we lift man above his nature more than above the earth he treads."

To "virtues," or positive qualities of which the power drive is in diverse ways capable, Hazlitt responded in full though troubled measure. Bromwich acutely reveals the parallels, and the mingling of admiration and ambivalence, in Hazlitt's commentaries on Shakespeare's Coriolanus, Milton's Satan, and Napoleon Bonaparte (in whose defense, vehement but qualified, Hazlitt published, at the end of his career, a four-volume *Life*). These are all persons of heroic will and power and of absolute self-reliance, who appeal to us in spite of—or rather, as Hazlitt recognizes, because of—their contempt for others who are less than themselves. There is a similar dividedness in his lifelong fascination with Edmund Burke, who is for Hazlitt the incomparable hero of prose, commanding "the most perfect prose-style, the most powerful, the most dazzling, the most daring." "The principle which guides his pen is . . . not pleasure, but power." "He exults in the display of power."

To Hazlitt, Burke is the unequaled master of eloquence not because he persuades us by rational argument, but because he overwhelms us, leaving us in a state of admiration and acquiescence that is independent of our conviction. Yet by putting the power of language in the service of established political power, as Hazlitt saw it, Burke was more than any other man responsible for the success of counterrevolution and the blasting of the highest human hope. "The consequences of his writings as instruments of political power have been tremendous, fatal, such as no exertion of wit, or knowledge, or genius can ever counteract or atone for." Nonetheless Hazlitt declares that "it has always been with me a test of the sense and candor of any one belonging to the opposite party, whether he allowed Burke to be a great man."

We also find this doubleness of assertion and attitude in Hazlitt's criticism of poetry. His highest praise is for the power of a poetic passage; yet he believed that the great poets (in our time one thinks of Yeats, Pound, Eliot), as well as the proclivities of the imagination that produce sublime poetry, naturally take the side of established hierarchy, glory, and power. "The cause of the people is indeed but little calculated as a subject for poetry. . . . The language of poetry naturally falls in with the language of power. The imagination is an exaggerating and exclusive faculty," and as opposed to the understanding, it is also an "aristocratical" faculty. "The principle of poetry is a very anti-levelling principle. . . . It is everything by excess."

Hazlitt's insight into the complex ways in which poets and poetry are involved with the social and political realities of power underlies what seems to me one of his most remarkable achievements in literary criticism, his discussion of Wordsworth's *Lyrical Ballads* in his late and best book, *The Spirit of the Age*. Hazlitt recognized that a social class structure was built into the traditional hierarchy and decorums of the poetic genres, in which the highest and most serious (epic and tragedy) represented kings and aristocracy in a language appropriate to their rank, and the descending genres were apportioned to a descending social order and idiom. This inherited class consciousness permeated the taste and sensibility of the middle- as well as upper-class readers in Wordsworth's time. In his early poetry, Wordsworth introduced the common, the lowly, the trivial, and the social outcast as subjects of serious, even tragic poetic concern, and in a language, he says, adopted from "humble and rustic life"; with the result, as Wordsworth complained, that his poems elicited "unremitting hostility," and "the slight, the aversion, and even the contempt" of its reviewers. Hazlitt interprets Wordsworth's originality in *Lyrical Ballads* as his egalitarian subversion of the implicit assumptions about class and power in poetry, and therefore as the equivalent in literature to the French Revolution in politics:

> It is one of the innovations of the time. It partakes of, and is carried along with, the revolutionary movement of our age: the political changes of the day were the model on which he formed and conducted his poetical experiments. His Muse . . . is a levelling one. It proceeds on a principle of equality. . . . His popular, inartificial style gets rid (at a blow) of all the trappings of verse, of all the high places of poetry. . . . Kings, queens, priests, robes, the altar and the throne . . . are not to be found here.

In this achievement, and in giving us "a new view of nature" by elevating the "mean," the "trivial," and the "insignificant" in the natural scene to the highest level of interest, Hazlitt asserts, Wordsworth is "the most original poet now living, and the one whose writings could the least be spared, for they have no substitute elsewhere."

Hazlitt, Keats remarked with admiration, "is your only good damner and if ever I am damn'd—damn me if I shouldn't like him to damn me." In a mood of pessimism Hazlitt wrote an essay, "On the Pleasure of Hating," in which he represents hatred, the "perverse . . . delight in mischief," as "the very spring of thought and action," which corrupts, and will continue to corrupt, society, religion, international relations, and one's relations to oneself. "We throw aside the trammels of civilization. . . . The wild beast resumes its sway within us," and "the heart rouses itself in its native lair, and utters a wild cry of joy, at being restored once more to freedom and lawless, unrestrained impulses." But to hate, as to power, Hazlitt gives a double interpretation and value; venting indignant hatred upon a subject that deserves it yields a proper and salutary pleasure at our verbal power both over our own feelings and over the subject that occasions them. The victim, as Hazlitt put it, "is no longer, in this case, the dupe." Toward those who had "maliciously and willfully blasted" the hopes vested by mankind in the French Revolution Hazlitt, consciously echoing Milton's Satan, had vowed "what we owe— hatred and scorn everlasting," and in expressing this hatred and scorn, Hazlitt achieved his most vehement, sustained, and comprehensive eloquence.

Bromwich quotes some splendid examples. Here is an additional instance of such rhetoric—a single, involved, and evolving sentence in which Hazlitt equals Burke in the power of his eloquence, but directs it against the entrenched political powers in whose defense Burke had misdirected his:

But there are persons of that low and inordinate appetite for servility, that they cannot be satisfied with any thing short of that sort of tyranny that has lasted for ever, and is likely to last for ever; that is strengthened and made desperate by the superstitions and prejudices of ages; that is enshrined in traditions, in laws, in usages, in the outward symbols of power, in the very idioms of language; that has struck its roots into the human heart, and clung round the human understanding like a nightshade; that overawes the imagination, and disarms the will to resist it, by the very enormity of the evil; that is cemented with gold and blood; guarded by reverence, guarded by power; linked in endless successions to the principle by which life is transmitted to the generations of tyrants and slaves, and destroying liberty with the first breath of life; that is absolute, unceasing, unerring, fatal, unutterable, abominable, monstrous.

Hazlitt, who liked to think of himself as a member of a party of one, then goes on, in this "Preface" to his *Political Essays*, even-handedly to demolish all the political parties of his time, the liberal Reformers and the Whigs no less than the Tories.

It is, however, Hazlitt's familiar essays that have always been the most widely read and will doubtless continue to be the most widely read. The form of most of these essays is distinctive, "Hazlittean." Bromwich notes, discerningly, that in his criticism Hazlitt differs from other major critics in that he does not use artistic unity as a prime criterion of literary value. In an essay on Charles Lamb, Thomas De Quincey, who was a highly conscious prose artist, depreciated Hazlitt because his thoughts are "discontinuous," lacking in "evolution" according to "the *law* of succession." Bromwich counters that the coherence of Hazlitt's thought is "associationist," which is true; although it should also be observed that Hazlitt's are often very free associations. He himself tells us that in writing his essays "I seldom see my way a page or even a sentence beforehand." His compositional unit is the single sentence; he piles sentence upon sentence, frequently according to no apparent principle of rhetorical order, into paragraphs three pages long; he is apt to change his topic abruptly and radically from one paragraph to the next; and when he reaches the end, he simply stops.

Hazlitt most approximates the norm of artistic unity in essays such as "My First Acquaintance with Poets," which have narrative sequence, but even that work ends in a conclusion in which nothing is concluded: "Enough of this for the present." Another narrative essay, "The Fight," however, is thoroughly ordered, and worth noting also as a reminder that, in addition to his merits as a critic of literature, oratory, painting, the theater, and politics, Hazlitt was both the originator and nonpareil of sports reporting. The essay describes the mounting excitement of the fans as they make their way to the appointed arena by stagecoach, with an overnight stop at an inn, then on foot; its central episode, the fight between the gas man and Bill Neate, is rendered in a tone that moves easily between the true heroic and the mock-heroic, and evolves through suspense, false expectation, and reversal to the denouement; it is followed by Hazlitt's sharing delighted reminiscences of the fight with others during the return home. It ends: "Toms called upon me the next day, to ask me if I did not think the fight was a complete thing? I said I thought it was. I hope he will relish my account of it." The essay is itself a complete thing, and reveals the kind of formal values that Hazlitt ordinarily gives up in order to achieve his own kind of essayistic brilliance, by his mastery of what he called "plain, point-blank speaking."

Hazlitt, himself an athlete, describes the elements and relations in his ideal of prose by a trope taken from athletic contests: "Every word should be a blow, every thought should instantly grapple with its fellow." When he is at his best in expressing the supple energy of his mind in the power of his prose, Hazlitt makes De Quincey's craftsmanship in the essay seem ponderous, Leigh Hunt's lightweight, and even Lamb's, in many instances, sequestered and quaint. There are moods of reading, in fact, in which no other essayist can give us the satisfaction that Hazlitt does. R. L. Stevenson said in one of his essays that "though we are mighty fine fellows nowadays, we cannot write like Hazlitt." David Bromwich, in the opening paragraph of his book about the other Hazlitt, cites this comment as appropriate to the standard Hazlitt, about whom he remarks that "I never cared for him much." I have a hunch, though, that even the other Hazlitt would have liked Stevenson's compliment very much.

ACKNOWLEDGMENTS

The author is grateful to his colleague Jonathan Culler for his suggestion that he collect and publish these essays, and for his acts of kindness and generosity over the years. Dianne Ferriss was, as always, an indispensable assistant in preparing the text for publication. Julia Reidhead, vice president at W. W. Norton & Company, was an enthusiastic supporter of the book, and Carly Fraser Doria, associate editor at Norton, was unfailingly expert and tactful as its editor. The author wishes also to thank the copyright holders for their generous permission to reprint the essays in this volume.

INDEX